Busy Mom's Lowfat Cookbook

Busy Mom's Lowfat Cookbook

*Healthful Family Dishes
the Kids Will Love
in 30 Minutes (or Less!)*

Elise M. Griffith

PRIMA PUBLISHING

PRIMA PUBLISHING and colophon are registered trademarks of Prima Communications, Inc.

Library of Congress Cataloging-in-Publication Data

Griffith, Elise M.
  Busy mom's lowfat cookbook: healthful family dishes the kids will
    love in 30 minutes (or less!) / Elise M. Griffith.
      p.   cm.
    Includes index.
    ISBN 0-7615-0614-4
    1. Lowfat diet—Recipes.   I. Title.
  RM237.7G75   1996
  641.5'638—dc20   96-29310
                                                                  CIP

96 97 98 99 00 01 AA 10 9 8 7 6 5 4 3 2 1
Printed in the United States of America

How to Order:

Single copies may be ordered from Prima Publishing, P.O. Box 1260BK, Rocklin, CA 95677; telephone (916) 632-4400. Quantity discounts are also available. On your letterhead, include information concerning the intended use of the books and the number of books you wish to purchase.

Nutritional Analyses:

A per serving nutritional breakdown is provided for each recipe. If a range is given for an ingredient amount, the breakdown is based on the smaller number. If a range is given for servings, the breakdown is based on the larger number. If a choice of ingredients is given in an ingredient listing, the breakdown is calculated using the first choice. Nutritional content may vary depending on the specific brands or types of ingredients used. "Optional" ingredients or those for which no specific amount is stated are not included in the breakdown. Nutritional figures are rounded to the nearest whole number.

Visit us online at http://www.primapublishing.com

Dedicated to my father,
James R. Parker,
who lovingly encouraged
my earliest culinary experiments.
Thank you, Pop!

Contents

Beating Brown-Bag Boredom   23

 A+ After-School Snacks   45

4 Soup's On!   67

7 What a Crock!   133

Bring On Dessert!   155

 Guess Who's Coming to Dinner?   177

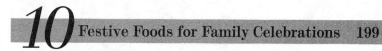

10 Festive Foods for Family Celebrations   199

Acknowledgments

Many thanks to my sainted husband, who tirelessly tasted and typed for me; I could not have done this without you. Special thanks to my young sons, who stayed out of trouble while Mommy was busy in the kitchen. To the many who shared tips, recipes, and encouragement—including Shawn Armstrong, Marlene Bellamy, Mary Black, Winnie Griffith, and Audrey Parker—I owe you more than I can ever repay. Special thanks to the gang at CompuServe's Online Services Development, who gleefully gobbled my "not quite ready for prime time" goodies. Thanks to my recipe testers, who let me know what worked and what didn't. And most of all, thank you Alice Anderson, Jennifer Basye Sander, Susan Silva, and Lisa Armstrong, my editors at Prima, along with the entire Prima staff.

Introduction

Kids have been doing battle at the dinner table for as long as . . . well, for as long as there have been toddlers! Those tiny tyrants are known for demanding cereal or hot dogs for breakfast, lunch, and dinner (until you think they'll turn into a hot dog), only to hurl the plate in disgust when you plop the 99th wiener in front of them. These are the unwritten laws of nature and children. Green foods are immediately suspect. The same child who picked at everything offered during mealtime for a week suddenly inhales three donuts in one sitting on Saturday morning. The little darling who just tucked carrots and green beans under the edge of her plate is sporting a sticky grin under a mountain of fruit-snack wrappers.

One reason why children choose junk food over dinner is that, frankly, the junk food often *tastes* better. Junk food is also more visually appealing to a kid than, say, pork chops. Burgers come wrapped in brightly colored paper, and you get a toy with your meal! Fruit snacks are Technicolor, sugary treats that look and taste like candy. They are candy; just read the label: there's more corn syrup than fruit juice in them. The thing is, kids need to be courted into eating healthier meals. Packaging, commercials, and peer pressure make the junk stuff irresistible.

As a busy parent, you're interested in recipes that are quick, easy to prepare, and nutritious. You also want entrées that your kids will eat! That's why so many of us cave in to burgers and pizza at the end of a long work day. I'm the first to admit that, when dinner time rolls around, I would sometimes rather head for the golden arches than head to the refrigerator. But what I want (and I suspect you do to) is to prepare quick, easy, appealing meals. And I know how. Impossible, you say? Hardly. That's what this book is all about. It's more than a cookbook. It's a book that is going to revive or ignite your love affair with cooking.

You don't need to be chained to the kitchen in order to concoct tempting—yet healthy—feasts for your family. Kids don't know how to cook. They don't *know* that the crunchy "fried" chicken and creamy sweet potatoes are low in fat and cholesterol. They'll never guess that the yummy fudge brownies are high in fiber and low in both sugar and fat. And since you whipped them up in less time than it takes to read the newspaper, mealtime is more enjoyable for everyone.

But dinner-table enjoyment goes beyond the entrée. A comfortable, pleasant atmosphere will make everything go down easier—and might even encourage more bites of green beans!

Kid Tips

- Variety is the spice of life—and the key to successful meals. Offering several dishes to choose from will help insure a balanced diet.

- Kids love color. Create colorful entrees, and use fun shapes (such as bow-tie pasta or crinkle-cut vegetables).

- Relax and enjoy each other. Children have a tough time sitting still; try engaging them in conversation, as this also helps distract them long enough to eat.

Some Facts About Fat

Fatty foods taste good. Greasy burgers, creamy gravy, gooey desserts—we love them all. There's a reason for that. Fat is *supposed* to be appealing. Why? Because long ago, when people toiled and labored to survive, they didn't have a neighborhood supermarket. Cold seasons were particularly difficult. Therefore, the limited amounts of food consumed had to pack enough calories to keep the body functioning during periods of famine and physical strain. Fatty foods are loaded with calories. By natural selection, those who consumed enough calories survived.

Today's society has it easier, yet Americans get about 38 percent of their daily calories from fat. This has led to obesity, heart disease, and certain types of cancer. Doctors and nutritional experts recommend that no more than 30 percent of daily calories come from fat.

All dietary fat is made up of saturated, monounsaturated, and polyunsaturated fatty acids. Saturated fats are believed to raise cholesterol levels and encourage the formation of plaque within the arteries. These fatty acids are found in meat, eggs, cheese, butter, cream, and tropical oils such as coconut, palm, and palm kernel oils. They're also believed to be created through the hydrogenation process of corn, canola, and other "safe" oils. Hydrogenating oil helps to preserve it, but it also renders the oil more saturated. It's a good idea to read labels, but there are some quick, painless ways to keep the "bad" fats out of your diet (at least in large quantities) and reduce the total amount of fat you consume each day.

Tips and Tricks for Cutting Fat from Favorite Recipes

• Use powdered skim milk in place of whole milk or cream when cooking and baking.

- Use reduced-fat cheese and nonfat cream cheese, and substitute nonfat yogurt for sour cream in recipes.

- Switch from oil to cooking sprays for sautés and fried foods.

- Substitute equal amounts of applesauce, puréed sweet potatoes, or fat-free mayonnaise for the oil or shortening in cakes, cookies, and baked treats.

- Trim excess fat from meats, and marinate for 15 minutes before cooking to assure moist meals.

- When oil is key to the recipe, use "light" canola or olive oil, but remember that olive oil smokes when the pan is too hot.

Lowfat cooking also means less mess and faster clean-up! There's nothing worse than finishing an enjoyable meal with the family and facing a mountain of greasy dishes. The good news is that the tools that help to reduce overall fat in your diet will also make your life easier.

Use Nonstick Cookware

The new nonstick pots and pans are far better than their flimsy 1970s ancestors, and you don't have to break your budget to buy some. Major department and discount stores carry a wide selection of coated cookware in every price range. Regal brand offers a low-end assortment of individual pieces, and some sets sell for as little as $40. Look for the heavier-weight pieces when purchasing any cookware, as the lighter, thinner pots and pans can warp over time.

Other good brands include Nordic Ware ($50 to $70 average set), Wear-Ever ($60 to $80 average set), Meyer ($60 to $130 average set), and T-Fal ($80 to $130 average set). You don't have to buy an entire set of cookware, however. You can easily make do with one each of the following: 8-inch and 10-inch frying pans; 1-quart and 2-quart saucepans; and lids. For easier preparation, or if you have a larger family, you might also want to purchase a stock pot, a griddle, and a 4- or 5-quart jumbo fryer (for stews and other dishes).

Invest in some plastic and wooden cooking utensils, since metal spoons, spatulas, and whisks will ruin nonstick pans. *Never* use steel wool pads on nonstick cookware. Instead, wash in warm, sudsy water with a wash cloth or plastic scouring pad, rinse, and dry. About once every month or so, place a drop of light canola oil in the bottom of each pan, and wipe carefully with a paper towel. This light oiling will keep the nonstick surface from drying and cracking.

Nonstick bakeware is also a good investment. Revere Ware makes an excellent set of nonstick products—complete with muffin tins, two cookie sheets, and a 9- × 13-inch cake pan—for as little as $40. You can also purchase individual pieces from Revere Ware. I recommend this company because their bakeware is made with insulated bottoms, which prevents excessive browning on the bottom of cookies, cakes, and muffins. As with any nonstick surface, use plastic or wooden utensils only.

Use a Microwave Oven Whenever You Can

I remember when my Pop brought home a huge package for my mother. She was puzzled when she unwrapped the odd-looking appliance—which was the size of a small television—and asked, "What am I supposed to do with this?"

"It's a microwave oven," he told her, "and you cook food in it. It takes half the time it would to prepare meals on the stove or in the electric oven!"

My mother saw the price tag ($400), and by the time we revived her, Pop had the new appliance on a cart of its own, ready to zap meals in minutes. Mom really did try to make use of her microwave oven, but almost 30 years of conventional cooking left her technologically challenged. "Baked" potatoes would be stiff or dry, meat turned an odd grayish-tan color (and was often too tough to chew), and her cheese-and-broccoli casserole came out black and smoking when she misread the instructions and cooked for 20 minutes on High. Within months, we had the most expensive coffee warmer in town.

Nowadays, microwave ovens are as common in households as automatic coffee-makers. And tiny, basic models can cost less than $100. My own "coffee-warmer" only set me back $70, but I do far more than warm coffee in it. Microwave ovens are great for any number of duties, including cooking vegetables without removing any of the nutritional value that traditional methods leach out. You can partially cook meats to reduce grilling time when you barbecue, and you can whip up desserts in a flash. Look for an appliance that has three-stage cooking and defrosting capabilities. Temperature probes, timers, and other extras are useful, but not essential.

Just about any glass or Pyrex plates, bowls, or bakeware can be used in a microwave oven. The products must have no metal handles or edges, however. Also look for Rubbermaid and Tupperware products that are designed exclusively for use in the microwave oven. Never grease or oil these products. If you want to insure nonstick performance, simply spray lightly with a cooking spray.

Fire Up the Grill

Aside from dinner at a restaurant, nothing is easier than grilling on the barbecue. If weather permits, make use of this lowfat way to cook as often as you like. Use leaner cuts of meat, and marinate for 15 minutes before grilling. Don't use oily marinades, however, and don't brush the meats with oil while you cook them. Additional oils are not only a fire hazard; they hamper your efforts to lower the level of fat in your diet.

For grilling, always be sure the coals are hot enough to cook the meat at the proper (and safe) temperatures, and be sure to cook all meat to be consumed by children until it is well done. Potentially fatal bacteria can lurk in a burger or pork chop. Also, be sure to use clean utensils. Do not place cooked meat on the same plate you brought it out on; either wash the plate or use a clean one.

There are all kinds of grills, from inexpensive aluminum patio models to fancy gas ones. If you plan to barbecue frequently during the year, it might be worth it to spend more money on a top-quality gas model. If you're only going to grill once or twice a month during the summer, then the least expensive model might be your best bet. Shop around. Also be sure to watch for the "end of season" sales around Labor Day. You can usually save more than 50 percent when you purchase at this time of year.

Slow-Cook Fast Dinners in a Crock-Pot

Of all of the gifts my husband has bought for me over the years, the most useful one has been a basic 4-quart Crock-Pot. I've used it so frequently that we're on our third one. Crock-Pots are marvelous for the busy parent; just toss everything into it at breakfast, turn it on Low, and dinner is guaranteed to be ready on time! Cleanup is also a snap, since your entire meal is cooked in one pot.

Virtually all Crock-Pots are affordable. You can get a low-end, one-piece unit that costs perhaps $15 (or less)—or you can get a larger, two-piece model with multiple temperature settings, automatic temperature adjustment, and other great features for about $40. Since I tend to wear out my Crock-Pots every few years, I get a budget version and it works just fine. I do recommend buying a reputable brand, such as Rival or West Bend.

I accidentally came upon a technique for getting moist results every time, even when using the leanest cuts of beef. When we were first married, I would thaw my roast or chicken overnight in the refrigerator, and then place it in the Crock-Pot in the morning. One day I forgot to thaw the meat. We were having company that night, and I'd planned to serve roast beef, which would simmer away while I was at work. So I took the frozen chunk of sirloin out of the wrapper and placed it in the bottom of the Crock-Pot. I quickly washed and assembled vegetables around the sides of it, covered the pot, turned it on Low, and hoped for the best. It was the juiciest roast I'd ever made. Now I routinely use frozen or partially frozen meats—being sure that they are thoroughly cooked before serving them.

Stocking Your Pantry

Finally, with a well-stocked pantry, you're always ready to rumba when supper time rolls around. Some staples to keep on hand in your kitchen include:

• cooking oil spray

• light canola or olive oil

• fat-free mayonnaise and salad dressings

• individual serving cups of applesauce (these are ½ cup servings, and perfect for baking)

• sweet potatoes (or 4-ounce jars of strained sweet-potato baby food)

- corn flakes
- bread crumbs
- instant rice
- thin spaghetti
- vegetable pastas
- quick-cooking oats
- canned kidney, pinto, and black beans
- canned, diced tomatoes
- canned vegetable broth
- whole wheat flour
- all-purpose flour
- rapid rising yeast
- baking powder
- corn starch
- powdered milk (pre-measured envelopes are the most convenient)
- spices and seasonings
- frozen vegetables and vegetable/pasta mixtures
- frozen apple and orange juice

Chapter 1

Speedy Breakfast or Lazy Brunch?

Whether you're rushing off to school and work, or spending time together on a weekend morning, breakfast is an important meal.

In most busy homes, breakfast consists of cold cereal and milk for the children, and a fast bit of toast and coffee for the harried parent. Even though we know the importance of a good breakfast, few of us have the time to cook in the morning, and the more "traditional" breakfast of eggs and bacon can leave a trail of grease in both the kitchen and our arteries.

Believe it or not, it's possible to prepare and eat a quick, nutritious breakfast every day. Some of the following recipes can be prepared the night before, giving you the opportunity to tap the "snooze" button. Other recipes are weekend favorites in my home. I hope they'll become favorites for your family, too.

Sunrise Ambrosia

Yield: 6 servings

Drain orange slices and pineapple chunks, and place in medium bowl. Peel and slice banana. Add to other fruit.

   Whisk together orange juice concentrate and honey; pour on fruit and toss. Sprinkle with coconut and serve.

ESTIMATED PREPARATION TIME: 5 minutes.

1 can (11 ounces) mandarin orange slices, in juice
1 can (8 ounces) pineapple chunks, in juice
1 medium banana
½ cup unsweetened frozen orange juice concentrate, thawed
¼ cup honey
¼ cup flaked coconut

158 Calories
1.4 g Protein
37.2 g Carbohydrates
1.5 g Fat
1.2 g Fiber
14 mg Sodium
0 mg Cholesterol

Breakfast Parfaits

Yield: 4 servings

2 cups lowfat aspartame-
  sweetened vanilla
  yogurt
1 dozen vanilla wafers,
  crushed
1 banana, sliced
1 cup fresh berries (or
  frozen berries,
  thawed), rinsed
4 vanilla wafers (for
  garnish)

Place a few tablespoons of vanilla yogurt in the bottom of each of 4 clear juice glasses. Sprinkle a tablespoon of crushed wafers over the yogurt. Add a few slices of banana and then a few berries. Top with a few more tablespoons of yogurt, and continue to layer until the cups are nearly full. Add a final layer of yogurt, and chill. Before serving, nestle a wafer on the top of each parfait.

ESTIMATED PREPARATION TIME: 5 minutes.

179 Calories
6.0 g Protein
38.4 g Carbohydrates
2.9 g Fat
1.6 g Fiber
124 mg Sodium
3 mg Cholesterol

Hot and Hearty Fruit Cups

Yield: 6 servings

Drain apricots and place in a medium-sized, microwavable bowl. Add cherry pie filling and raisins. Mix thoroughly. Microwave on highest setting for 3 minutes.

Combine all remaining ingredients in a small bowl. Place hot fruit in individual serving bowls, sprinkle with topping, and serve.

ESTIMATED PREPARATION TIME: 10 minutes.

ESTIMATED COOKING TIME: 3 minutes.

1 can (17 ounces) apricot halves, in juice
1 can (21 ounces) "lite" aspartame-sweetened cherry pie filling
½ cup raisins
½ teaspoon cinnamon
2 tablespoons brown sugar
½ cup wheat germ

198 Calories
1.5 g Protein
49.2 g Carbohydrates
0.4 g Fat
1.4 g Fiber
29 mg Sodium
0 mg Cholesterol

Quick and Hearty Muesli

Yield: 4 servings

2 cups lowfat granola
½ cup dried berries
½ cup nonfat aspartame-
   sweetened vanilla
   yogurt
½ cup skim milk

Combine all ingredients in microwavable bowl or casserole dish, stirring to coat evenly. Cover and microwave on High for 2 minutes. Stir, place in individual serving bowls, and serve.

ESTIMATED PREPARATION TIME: 3 minutes.

ESTIMATED COOKING TIME: 2 minutes.

306 Calories
7.4 g Protein
63.6 g Carbohydrates
3.1 g Fat
6.0 g Fiber
163 mg Sodium
1 mg Cholesterol

Oatmeal Swirl

Yield: 4 servings

In a medium pot, bring water to a low boil. Add the oats and salt, stir, and cook for 1 minute. Set aside.

Stir together applesauce, cinnamon, and syrup.

Spoon oatmeal into 4 bowls. Place a dollop of the applesauce mixture into the center of each. Using the handle end of a spoon, create swirls by dragging the tip through the applesauce and oatmeal. Do not stir.

3 cups water
1½ cups quick-cooking oats
¼ teaspoon salt
½ cup applesauce
¼ teaspoon cinnamon
2 tablespoons "lite"
  maple-flavored syrup

ESTIMATED PREPARATION TIME: 6 minutes.

ESTIMATED COOKING TIME: 2 minutes.

VARIATIONS

Berry Oatmeal Swirl: substitute strawberry jam for applesauce.

Peaches and Cream Oatmeal Swirl: substitute lowfat peach-flavored yogurt (mixed with 1 tablespoon honey) for applesauce.

157 Calories
5.0 g Protein
30.5 g Carbohydrates
2.0 g Fat
3.8 g Fiber
141 mg Sodium
0 mg Cholesterol

Milk and Honey Breakfast

Yield: 4 servings

1½ cups skim milk
¼ cup honey
1 cup quick-cooking
  Cream of Wheat
  cereal
1 cup fresh berries, rinsed

Pour milk and honey into a microwavable bowl. Microwave on High for 90 seconds. Stir in dry cereal and mix well. Microwave on High for 2 to 3 minutes. Stir and allow to sit for a few minutes.

Spoon into individual bowls, top with berries, and serve.

ESTIMATED PREPARATION TIME: 5 minutes.

ESTIMATED COOKING TIME: 5 minutes.

269 Calories
8.1 g Protein
57.2 g Carbohydrates
0.9 g Fat
1.0 g Fiber
52 mg Sodium
2 mg Cholesterol

Busy Mom's Lowfat Cookbook

Hawaiian Breakfast Pizzas

Yield: 4 servings

Preheat oven to 350 degrees. Arrange English muffins on ungreased cookie sheet. Lay strips of ham across the top of each muffin, checkerboard style. Top with a slice of pineapple, and then a slice of cheese. Bake for 5 minutes, or until the cheese has melted slightly.

2 whole wheat English muffins, split
2 thin slices lean ham (cold cuts work well), cut into thin strips
4 pineapple slices
4 slices reduced-fat American cheese

ESTIMATED PREPARATION TIME: 5 minutes.

ESTIMATED COOKING TIME: 5 minutes.

139 Calories
6.9 g Protein
20.9 g Carbohydrates
3.7 g Fat
1.5 g Fiber
481 mg Sodium
12 mg Cholesterol

In-a-Flash Ham and Cheese "Omelet"

Yield: 4 servings

2 containers (4 ounces each) egg substitute
salt and pepper
1 package (3 ounces) thin-sliced turkey ham
1 cup shredded fat-free Cheddar cheese
2 tablespoons frozen chopped onion (or 1 tablespoon dried minced onion)
¼ teaspoon parsley flakes

Pour egg substitute into large microwavable casserole dish that has been lightly coated with cooking oil spray. Sprinkle with salt and pepper if desired. Chop turkey ham into ½-inch pieces and sprinkle over egg substitute. Sprinkle cheese over the ham, and follow with the onion and parsley flakes. Cover and microwave on Medium High for 3 minutes. Allow to sit for an additional 2 to 3 minutes.

ESTIMATED PREPARATION TIME: 5 minutes.

ESTIMATED COOKING TIME: 3 minutes.

95 Calories
18.1 g Protein
2.5 g Carbohydrates
1.1 g Fat
0.1 g Fiber
495 mg Sodium
32 mg Cholesterol

Farmer's Scramble

Yield: 4 servings

Combine all ingredients except the cheese in a microwavable casserole dish that has been lightly coated with cooking oil spray. Sprinkle with cheese. Cover and microwave on High for 3 minutes or until eggs begin to set. Allow to sit for an additional 2 to 3 minutes before serving.

ESTIMATED PREPARATION TIME: 10 minutes.

ESTIMATED COOKING TIME: 3 minutes.

1 can (16 ounces) sliced new potatoes, drained
½ cup diced green onions
¼ cup diced green pepper
6 cherry tomatoes, quartered
1 container (4 ounces) egg substitute (or 4 eggs, beaten)
½ cup reduced-fat shredded Cheddar cheese

105 Calories
8.0 g Protein
12.8 g Carbohydrates
2.8 g Fat
0.9 g Fiber
412 mg Sodium
10 mg Cholesterol

Breakfast Pockets

Yield: 4 servings

1 carton (4 ounces) egg substitute (or 4 eggs, beaten)

½ cup leftover turkey ham, diced

4 slices reduced-fat American or Cheddar cheese

4 whole wheat pitas, with 1 inch trimmed from one edge to form pocket

Preheat a nonstick skillet over medium-low heat. Lightly coat the skillet with cooking oil spray and pour in egg substitute, tossing in diced ham as the egg mixture begins to set.

Place a slice of cheese in each pita pocket. Spoon an equal portion of egg mixture into each pocket, and serve.

ESTIMATED PREPARATION TIME: 4 minutes.

ESTIMATED COOKING TIME: 4 minutes.

248 Calories
19.5 g Protein
24.4 g Carbohydrates
7.8 g Fat
3.0 g Fiber
677 mg Sodium
42 mg Cholesterol

Bird in the Nest

Yield: 4 servings

Preheat nonstick griddle over low heat. Using a small drinking glass, cut a circle out of the center of each slice of bread, and set aside.

Lightly spray the griddle with cooking oil spray, place a slice or two of the bread onto the griddle, and crack an egg over each "hole," pouring egg into the "hole." Sprinkle with salt and pepper.

As the egg begins to set up, carefully turn once with a spatula. When the eggs are cooked, place on individual plates.

ESTIMATED PREPARATION TIME: 5 minutes.

ESTIMATED COOKING TIME: 5 minutes.

4 slices whole wheat
   bread
4 medium eggs
   salt and pepper

118 Calories
8.1 g Protein
8.9 g Carbohydrates
5.6 g Fat
1.3 g Fiber
173 mg Sodium
213 mg Cholesterol

Breakfast Muffins

Yield: 12 muffins

1 cup reduced-fat biscuit
  mix
½ cup quick-cooking oats
¼ teaspoon cinnamon
2 egg whites (or ¼ cup
  egg substitute), lightly
  beaten
1 tablespoon canola oil
½ cup nonfat plain yogurt
½ cup unsweetened
  orange juice
  concentrate, thawed
1 cup raisins (or chopped
  dried fruit)

Place paper muffin cups in a microwavable muffin pan. In a large bowl, stir together biscuit mix, oats, and cinnamon. Add egg whites, oil, yogurt, and juice concentrate. Blend, but do not over-mix. Batter will be slightly lumpy. Fold in raisins.

Fill muffin cups two-thirds full. Sprinkle a little cinnamon on top of each muffin, if desired. Microwave on Medium High for 2 minutes. Rotate muffin pan. Microwave on Medium High for an additional 2 to 3 minutes. Allow to cool.

Note: These muffins can be frozen and reheated in the microwave oven.

ESTIMATED PREPARATION TIME: 5 minutes.

ESTIMATED COOKING TIME: 5 minutes.

HIGH ALTITUDE NOTE: Add 1 tablespoon flour.

124 Calories
3.1 g Protein
24.2 g Carbohydrates
2.1 g Fat
1.2 g Fiber
133 mg Sodium
0 mg Cholesterol

Make-Ahead Yam Breakfast Bars

Yield: 12 bars

Preheat oven to 425 degrees. Purée entire contents of can of yams in a blender or food processor. Pour into a large mixing bowl. Stir in cinnamon. Add egg whites and sugar. Beat until smooth.

In a small bowl, combine flour, baking soda, and a pinch of salt. Add slowly to the yam mixture, beating until smooth and creamy. Fold in cereal, and stir until well mixed.

Spread into a 13- × 9-inch pan that has been lightly coated with cooking oil spray. Bake for 20 minutes. Remove from oven, cool, and cut into 3-inch squares.

Note: Bars can be refrigerated for up to one week.

1 can (29 ounces) cut yams in light syrup
¼ teaspoon cinnamon
2 egg whites, slightly beaten
¼ cup light brown sugar
1½ cups all-purpose flour
1 teaspoon baking soda
salt
3 cups lowfat granola with raisins

ESTIMATED PREPARATION TIME: 10 minutes.

ESTIMATED COOKING TIME: 20 minutes.

HIGH ALTITUDE NOTE: Add 2 tablespoons flour, and increase oven temperature to 450 degrees.

250 Calories
4.7 g Protein
54.5 g Carbohydrates
1.9 g Fat
3.2 g Fiber
176 mg Sodium
0 mg Cholesterol

Make-Ahead Banana-Split Breakfast Bars

Yield: 9 bars

1½ cups reduced-fat biscuit mix
¾ cup nonfat aspartame-sweetened vanilla yogurt
¼ cup honey
3 ripe bananas, mashed
½ cup semisweet chocolate chips (or carob chips)
½ cup chopped pecans
9 maraschino cherries

Preheat oven to 375 degrees. Combine biscuit mix, yogurt, honey, and banana in a large mixing bowl. Stir in chocolate chips and pecans.

Lightly coat a 9-inch square cake pan with cooking oil spray. Pour batter into pan. Arrange cherries on top in three rows of three.

Bake for 20 minutes. Remove from oven, cover with foil, and cool overnight.

ESTIMATED PREPARATION TIME: 10 minutes.

ESTIMATED COOKING TIME: 20 minutes.

HIGH ALTITUDE NOTE: Add 2 tablespoons flour.

249 Calories
3.6 g Protein
41.2 g Carbohydrates
9.1 g Fat
1.6 g Fiber
244 mg Sodium
1 mg Cholesterol

Busy Mom's Lowfat Cookbook

Bunny Breakfast Muffins

Yield: 12 muffins

Preheat oven to 400 degrees. In a large bowl, combine all dry ingredients and stir. Purée carrots. Add carrots, oil, and orange juice concentrate to dry ingredients and blend well. Fold in raisins.

Place paper muffin cups in muffin pan. Using an ice cream scoop, drop one generous scoop of batter into each cup. Bake for 15 minutes.

Note: These muffins can be prepared the night before, covered with foil, and allowed to cool for out-the-door convenience in the morning.

1 cup flour
½ cup quick-cooking oats
2 teaspoons baking powder
¼ teaspoon cinnamon
1 can (16 ounces) sliced carrots, drained
1 tablespoon canola oil
½ cup unsweetened orange juice concentrate, thawed
½ cup raisins

ESTIMATED PREPARATION TIME: 10 minutes.

ESTIMATED COOKING TIME: 15 minutes.

HIGH ALTITUDE NOTE: Add 2 tablespoons flour, and reduce baking powder to 1 teaspoon.

76 Calories
1.4 g Protein
15.1 g Carbohydrates
1.5 g Fat
1.0 g Fiber
114 mg Sodium
0 mg Cholesterol

Peanut Butter and Jelly Breakfast Rolls

Yield: 8 rolls

1 can (7½ ounces)
   refrigerated crescent
   roll dough
8 teaspoons reduced-fat
   peanut butter
8 teaspoons all-fruit
   spread (any flavor)

Preheat oven to 425 degrees. Unroll crescent dough. Spread each triangle with 1 teaspoon peanut butter and 1 teaspoon jelly, and roll up. Place on nonstick cookie sheet, and bake for 8 to 10 minutes.

ESTIMATED PREPARATION TIME: 5 minutes.

ESTIMATED COOKING TIME: 10 minutes.

134 Calories
3.4 g Protein
19.0 g Carbohydrates
5.0 g Fat
0.6 g Fiber
362 mg Sodium
0 mg Cholesterol

"Sourdough" Flapjacks with Cinnamon-Apple Topping

Yield: 12 pancakes

Place flour, baking powder, and salt in a large bowl, and stir.

In a separate small bowl, combine egg, yogurt, milk, and water. Pour over dry ingredients and whisk until smooth and free of lumps. Set aside.

Preheat a nonstick griddle or skillet over medium heat. Just before cooking, spray very lightly with cooking oil spray.

Using a soup ladle, pour batter onto the heated griddle or pan. Turn as bubbles begin to form and pop on the surface of the pancake.

For Topping: Combine all ingredients in a microwavable bowl. Heat in microwave oven on High for 2 minutes. Serve immediately over hot pancakes.

2 cups all-purpose flour
1 teaspoon baking powder
¼ teaspoon salt
1 egg
½ cup nonfat plain yogurt
1 cup skim milk
½ cup water

Topping
1½ cups applesauce
½ cup "lite" maple-flavored syrup
¼ teaspoon cinnamon

ESTIMATED PREPARATION TIME: 10 minutes.

ESTIMATED COOKING TIME: 15 minutes.

HIGH ALTITUDE NOTE: Reduce baking powder to ½ teaspoon.

(with topping)
142 Calories
3.9 g Protein
29.9 g Carbohydrates
0.7 g Fat
1.1 g Fiber
95 mg Sodium
18 mg Cholesterol

Carolina Corn Cakes

Yield: 10 corn cakes

1 package (8½ ounces)
    corn muffin mix
2 tablespoons flour
2 egg whites
½ cup skim milk
1 cup canned creamed
    corn
1 package (12 ounces)
    frozen berries
¼ cup sugar

Preheat a nonstick griddle over medium-low heat. In a large bowl, combine muffin mix, flour, egg whites, and milk. Blend well. Fold in corn.

Spray the surface of the griddle lightly with cooking oil spray. Using a soup ladle, pour batter onto griddle surface. Turn when bubbles appear and edges begin to set.

Place berries and sugar in a microwavable bowl, cover, and heat on High for 2 minutes. Stir. Heat on High for an additional 2 to 3 minutes, or until berries start to bubble. Spoon over corn cakes.

ESTIMATED PREPARATION TIME: **10 minutes.**

ESTIMATED COOKING TIME: **15 minutes.**

HIGH ALTITUDE NOTE: **Add 1 tablespoon flour, and cook over medium heat rather than medium-low heat.**

146 Calories
3.7 g Protein
34.0 g Carbohydrates
0.3 g Fat
2.7 g Fiber
458 mg Sodium
0 mg Cholesterol

Busy Mom's Lowfat Cookbook

Lemon Poppy-Seed Pancakes

Yield: 10 to 12 pancakes

Preheat nonstick griddle over medium-low heat. Place dry ingredients in a large bowl and stir to combine. Add egg, yogurt, lemonade concentrate, and water. Mix until well combined.

Lightly coat griddle with cooking oil spray. Using soup ladle, pour batter onto griddle. Turn when bubbles appear and begin to pop on the surface.

Sprinkle with powdered sugar and serve.

1½ cups flour
2 teaspoons baking powder
¼ teaspoon salt
1 tablespoon poppy seeds
1 egg
½ cup nonfat aspartame-sweetened lemon yogurt
¼ cup frozen lemonade concentrate, thawed
½ cup cold water
powdered sugar

ESTIMATED PREPARATION TIME: 5 minutes.

ESTIMATED COOKING TIME: 15 minutes.

HIGH ALTITUDE NOTE: Reduce baking powder to 1 teaspoon.

98 Calories
2.7 g Protein
19.6 g Carbohydrates
0.9 g Fat
0.5 g Fiber
112 mg Sodium
17 mg Cholesterol

Grizzly Bear Pancakes

Yield: 10 pancakes

1 package (8½ ounces) bran-and-date muffin mix
1 egg
½ cup nonfat plain yogurt
½ cup skim milk

Preheat nonstick griddle over medium-low heat. Place all ingredients in medium bowl and mix together until well combined.

Lightly coat griddle with cooking spray. Using soup ladle, pour batter onto griddle. Turn when bubbles appear and begin to pop on the surface.

Note: Serve with dark molasses or maple syrup.

ESTIMATED PREPARATION TIME: 3 minutes.

ESTIMATED COOKING TIME: 15 minutes.

HIGH ALTITUDE NOTE: Add 1 tablespoon flour; cook over medium heat rather than medium-low heat.

92 Calories
3.8 g Protein
15.2 g Carbohydrates
1.1 g Fat
1.1 g Fiber
189 mg Sodium
22 mg Cholesterol

Busy Mom's Lowfat Cookbook

Chapter 2

Beating Brown-Bag Boredom

Simple Submarine
Sandwiches

Kangaroo Pizza
Sandwiches

King Triton's Pockets

Angel Mitts

Three-Ring Sandwiches

Brown-Bag "Burritos"

Portable Lunch Kabobs

Lunch-Box Chicken
Quesadillas

Better Than Lunchables

Barbecued "Beef"
Sandwiches

Grilled Cheese Cut-Outs

Fiesta Taco Dogs

Biscuit Burgers

Pasta Wheels and
"Meatballs"

Easy Chicken Nuggets

Quick Chicken and
Dumplings

Quick Macaroni and
Cheese

Hot Dog Kabobs

Cracker Pizza

Quick Straw-and-Hay

Like many busy moms, I've prepared hundreds of peanut-butter-and-jelly (PBJ) sandwiches. They're quick and easy, and I know my children will eat them. For a long time, I soothed my guilty conscience by handing them each a vitamin tablet with lunch, figuring that it might balance the sandwich, potato chips, and "fruit flavored" drink they gobbled with glee.

It seemed to me that unless I served PBJs or other low-nutrition favorites (kiddy hamburger meals, frozen pizza, canned pasta, etc.), lunch time could become whine time—until I began to play with food. Cookie cutters, unconventional sandwich breads, and whimsical mixtures worked magic on our mid-day meals. I also discovered that I could create healthy substitutes for convenience foods.

The following recipes include packable, portable, brown bag basics—plus fast hot lunches for the home crew.

Simple Submarine Sandwiches

Yield: 4 sandwiches

Combine salad dressing and mustard, and spread on hot dog buns. Place shredded lettuce on each bun and layer meat slices on top. Cut cheese slices in half and place a half slice on each sandwich. Close, cut, and serve with fresh fruit.

ESTIMATED PREPARATION TIME: 5 minutes.

2 tablespoons reduced-fat salad dressing

2 teaspoons prepared mustard

4 whole wheat hot dog buns

3 large fancy lettuce leaves, shredded fine

1 package (4 ounces) thin-sliced beef salami

1 package (4 ounces) thin-sliced turkey ham

2 slices fat-free American cheese

322 Calories
19.9 g Protein
30.8 g Carbohydrates
13.0 g Fat
2.1 g Fiber
1261 mg Sodium
55 mg Cholesterol

Kangaroo Pizza Sandwiches

Yield: 4 sandwiches

4 whole wheat pitas
  lettuce leaves
4 slices part-skim
  mozzarella cheese
½ pound smoked turkey
  sausage, sliced thin
1 large tomato, diced

Cut pitas in half to form half-circle pockets. Line with lettuce leaves. Slide in a slice of mozzarella, some sausage slices, and a tablespoon or two of tomatoes.

Note: If you wish, omit the lettuce and heat the sandwiches in the microwave oven for a few seconds to melt the cheese.

ESTIMATED PREPARATION TIME: 5 minutes.

252 Calories
16.8 g Protein
26.0 g Carbohydrates
8.5 g Fat
3.4 g Fiber
637 mg Sodium
31 mg Cholesterol

Busy Mom's Lowfat Cookbook

King Triton's Pockets

Yield: 4 to 6 servings

In a medium bowl, combine all ingredients except the bread and lettuce, and mix well. Line pita pockets with lettuce leaves if desired, and fill with the seafood mixture.

Note: For best results, place each sandwich in a sealable container rather than in a fold-over sandwich bags.

ESTIMATED PREPARATION TIME: 10 minutes.

½ cup diced imitation crab meat
1 can (6 ounces) tuna in water, drained
1 tablespoon sweet pickle relish
1 tablespoon finely chopped green onion
2 tablespoons fat-free plain yogurt
1 tablespoon reduced-fat salad dressing
⅛ teaspoon black pepper
4 to 6 whole wheat pita breads, cut in half
lettuce leaves

200 Calories
14.5 g Protein
27.9 g Carbohydrates
3.0 g Fat
3.3 g Fiber
481 mg Sodium
9 mg Cholesterol

Angel Mitts

Yield: 4 servings

1 container (8 ounces) nonfat soft cream cheese

1 can (4 ounces) crushed pineapple in juice, drained

¼ cup low-salt dry-roasted peanuts

4 whole wheat pita breads, trimmed at the top to form the shape of a baseball mitt

In a small bowl, combine cream cheese and pineapple. Mix well. Place the peanuts in a paper bag, fold the top securely, and crush using a rolling pin or coffee can. Add to the cream cheese mixture and blend lightly. Spread mixture into pita "mitts."

ESTIMATED PREPARATION TIME: 10 minutes.

224 Calories
14.9 g Protein
27.4 g Carbohydrates
5.2 g Fat
3.4 g Fiber
566 mg Sodium
10 mg Cholesterol

Three-Ring Sandwiches

Yield: 4 servings

Using the top edge of a clean drinking glass, cut the cheese and meat into circles that are the approximate diameter of the bagels. Blot the pineapple slices with paper towels to eliminate excess moisture. Spread the bagels with salad dressing, and assemble each sandwich.

ESTIMATED PREPARATION TIME: 5 minutes.

VARIATION: These sandwiches can be heated to melt cheese: place in 350 degree oven for 5 minutes.

4 slices reduced-fat American cheese
4 slices turkey breast lunch meat
4 pineapple slices, drained
2 tablespoons reduced-fat salad dressing
4 multi-grain bagels, sliced

347 Calories
17.7 g Protein
57.9 g Carbohydrates
6.0 g Fat
2.7 g Fiber
1087 mg Sodium
17 mg Cholesterol

Brown-Bag "Burritos"

Yield: 4 servings

1 can (6 ounces) chunk
   chicken, drained
1 tablespoon fat-free
   mayonnaise
1 teaspoon lemon juice
4 flour tortillas
¼ cup chopped green
   onions
1 medium tomato, diced
½ cup reduced-fat
   shredded Cheddar
   cheese

In a small bowl, combine chicken, mayonnaise, and lemon juice. Steam the tortillas between damp paper towels in the microwave oven for easier handling. Spread the chicken mix in the center of each tortilla. Top with onions, tomato, and Cheddar cheese. Fold the bottom edge of the tortilla up, and roll the sides tightly to form a burrito. Place burrito in a sandwich bag and seal.

ESTIMATED PREPARATION TIME: 7 minutes.

217 Calories
15.9 g Protein
20.5 g Carbohydrates
8.6 g Fat
1.4 g Fiber
423 mg Sodium
40 mg Cholesterol

Busy Mom's Lowfat Cookbook

Portable Lunch Kabobs

Yield: 4 servings

Alternate cheese, meat, tomatoes, and pineapple chunks on wooden skewers. Wrap in foil or plastic wrap before packing in lunch box. Serve with wheat crackers and salad.

ESTIMATED PREPARATION TIME: 10 minutes.

4 ounces reduced-fat Cheddar cheese, cubed

4 ounces cubed turkey ham or smoked sausage

1 pint cherry tomatoes, rinsed, with stems removed

1 can (16 ounces) pineapple chunks in juice, drained

221 Calories
14.8 g Protein
27.1 g Carbohydrates
6.9 g Fat
1.9 g Fiber
505 mg Sodium
56 mg Cholesterol

Lunch-Box Chicken Quesadillas

Yield: 4 servings

8 whole wheat flour
tortillas
½ cup reduced-fat
shredded Cheddar
cheese
½ cup reduced-fat
shredded Monterey
Jack cheese
1 can (6 ounces) chunk
chicken, drained
¼ cup diced green onions

Lay a paper towel on a microwavable plate. Place a tortilla on the paper towel. Sprinkle with each of the cheeses, some chicken, and onions. Lay another tortilla on top and cover with a paper towel. Place another tortilla on top of that paper towel, and repeat the process. Continue until 4 quesadillas have been assembled.

Microwave on High for 2 minutes. Allow to cool. Slice into wedges and wrap in sandwich bags. Serve with fruit cups and vegetable crudités.

ESTIMATED PREPARATION TIME: 5 minutes.

ESTIMATED COOKING TIME: 2 minutes.

432 Calories
25.4 g Protein
51.4 g Carbohydrates
17.2 g Fat
2.1 g Fiber
920 mg Sodium
50 mg Cholesterol

Busy Mom's Lowfat Cookbook

Better Than Lunchables

Yield: 1 serving

Bundle crackers, cheese, ham, grapes, and carrot sticks separately (similar to the commercial varieties). Place in a thermal lunch bag.

ESTIMATED PREPARATION TIME: 5 minutes.

6 Rye Toast crackers
2 slices reduced-fat
    Swiss cheese, cut into
    3 pieces each
2 thin slices lean ham, cut
    into 3 pieces each
1 small bunch red seedless
    grapes
3 to 4 carrot sticks

352 Calories
24.5 g Protein
45.3 g Carbohydrates
12.3 g Fat
11.6 g Fiber
884 mg Sodium
40 mg Cholesterol

Barbecued "Beef" Sandwiches

Yield: 4 servings

2 cups frozen ground beef
  substitute (such as
  Harvest Burgers For
  Recipes)
½ cup mild barbecue
  sauce
1 small tomato, diced
4 whole wheat buns

Combine meat substitute, barbecue sauce, and tomatoes in a microwavable baking dish. Microwave on High for 3 to 5 minutes, or until hot and bubbling. Spoon mixture onto buns. Serve with salad and fruit.

ESTIMATED PREPARATION TIME: 5 minutes.

ESTIMATED COOKING TIME: 5 minutes.

357 Calories
19.0 g Protein
52.4 g Carbohydrates
7.1 g Fat
6.4 g Fiber
923 mg Sodium
0 mg Cholesterol

Busy Mom's Lowfat Cookbook

Grilled Cheese Cut-Outs

Yield: 6 sandwiches

Lay out bread slices on a cutting board. Using cookie cutters, cut shapes out of the bread (2 of each shape for each sandwich). Repeat with the cheese slices, but cut only one shape per sandwich.

Spread the bread slices with mayonnaise on alternating sides (the sides that will be grilled). Preheat a nonstick skillet over low heat. Set one side of each sandwich on the heated surface, mayonnaise-side down. Carefully align the matching cut-out of cheese on each, and top with another prepared slice of bread in its matching design, mayonnaise-side up.

Grill until lightly browned. Turn and grill for an additional moment to brown underside. Serve with salad and fruit.

12 slices whole wheat bread
6 slices reduced-fat American cheese
3 tablespoons fat-free mayonnaise

ESTIMATED PREPARATION TIME: 5 minutes.

ESTIMATED COOKING TIME: 10 minutes.

113 Calories
7.4 g Protein
20.3 g Carbohydrates
1.1 g Fat
2.6 g Fiber
539 mg Sodium
0 mg Cholesterol

Fiesta Taco Dogs

Yield: 4 servings

4 fat-free wieners
½ cup chili con carne
4 taco shells
¼ head lettuce, shredded
1 tomato, diced
½ cup reduced-fat
    shredded Cheddar
    cheese

Boil the wieners in a small pot of water over medium heat. Place chili con carne in a small saucepan, and heat on low, stirring occasionally. Remove wieners from water. Using a fork and sharp knife, slice wieners in half lengthwise.

Place 2 wiener halves in each taco shell. Spoon on approximately 2 tablespoons of hot chili. Sprinkle lettuce, tomatoes, and cheese over the meat and chili.

ESTIMATED PREPARATION TIME: 10 minutes.

ESTIMATED COOKING TIME: 10 minutes.

179 Calories
13.8 g Protein
13.1 g Carbohydrates
5.9 g Fat
1.9 g Fiber
897 mg Sodium
27 mg Cholesterol

Busy Mom's Lowfat Cookbook

Biscuit Burgers and Fries

Yield: 4 to 6 servings

Preheat oven to 400 degrees. Place potatoes in a large clean paper bag, add cornstarch and salt, fold top over to seal, and shake vigorously. Spread coated potatoes on a nonstick cookie sheet and bake for 15 minutes.

Preheat a large nonstick skillet over medium heat. Form ground beef into 2-inch balls. Place a sheet of waxed paper on working surface and arrange meat balls. Lay another sheet of waxed paper over the meatballs and press to flatten. Place the mini-burgers in the pre-heated skillet and sprinkle with onion salt and pepper. Cook for 2 to 3 minutes, and turn.

Arrange biscuits in a 9-inch square cake pan that has been lightly coated with cooking oil spray. Bake for 10 minutes. Cool slightly. Cut biscuits in half, place a burger on each, and serve with French fries and condiments.

1 package (16 ounces) frozen shoestring potatoes
½ cup cornstarch
1 teaspoon salt
1 pound extra-lean ground beef
onion salt and pepper
1 can (7½ ounces) refrigerated biscuits

ESTIMATED PREPARATION TIME: 10 minutes.

ESTIMATED COOKING TIME: 20 minutes.

446 Calories
21.1 g Protein
50.1 g Carbohydrates
17.8 g Fat
2.9 g Fiber
865 mg Sodium
54 mg Cholesterol

Pasta Wheels and "Meatballs"

Yield: 8 servings

boiling water (quantity per package directions)
1 cup packaged hamburger substitute mix
2 cups vegetable pasta wheels
½ cup unseasoned bread crumbs
½ teaspoon Italian seasoning
1 egg white
1 can or jar (26–27 ounces) spaghetti sauce

In a large bowl, add boiling water to hamburger substitute; stir and set aside to cool. Cook pasta, drain, and set aside.

Add bread crumbs, Italian seasoning, and egg white to meat substitute mixture. Mix all ingredients thoroughly; the mixture should be pasty. Prepare a nonstick frying pan with a light coating of cooking spray. Form 1-inch balls with the mixture, and brown over medium heat, turning frequently.

Place cooked pasta, spaghetti sauce, and "meat" balls in a 2- or 3-quart pot, and simmer over low heat for 10 minutes.

ESTIMATED PREPARATION TIME: 20 minutes.

ESTIMATED COOKING TIME: 30 minutes.

215 Calories
7.8 g Protein
39.0 g Carbohydrates
3.2 g Fat
2.9 g Fiber
466 mg Sodium
0 mg Cholesterol

Easy Chicken Nuggets

Yield: 4 servings

Preheat oven to 425 degrees. Soak chicken cubes in salted ice water for 5 minutes. Place muffin mix, paprika, and pepper in a plastic bag. Remove a few chicken cubes from the ice water, drop in the bag with the corn mixture, and shake to coat. Place coated chicken cubes on a nonstick cookie sheet. Repeat until all cubes are coated and arranged on the cookie sheet.

Bake for 12 minutes. Serve with Honey Mustard Dip (recipe below).

Honey Mustard Dip: Mix ingredients together in a small bowl and use for dipping.

1 pound boneless, skinless chicken breasts, cubed
1 package (7½ ounces) corn muffin mix
1 teaspoon paprika
¼ teaspoon pepper

Honey Mustard Dip
⅓ cup Dijon mustard
3 tablespoons honey

ESTIMATED PREPARATION TIME: 10 minutes.

ESTIMATED COOKING TIME: 12 minutes.

ESTIMATED PREPARATION TIME: 2 minutes for Honey Mustard Dip.

295 Calories
30.0 g Protein
39.9 g Carbohydrates
1.5 g Fat
3.6 g Fiber
882 mg Sodium
65 mg Cholesterol

Quick Chicken and Dumplings

Yield: 4 to 6 servings

1½ cups cooked chicken
    meat, diced
1 can (16 ounces) mixed
    vegetables
1 cup water
2 teaspoons chicken
    bouillon granules
    (or 2 cubes)
1 tablespoon cornstarch
1 can (7½ ounces)
    refrigerated biscuits

Place chicken, entire contents of canned vegetables, water, and bouillon in a large nonstick skillet and cook over medium heat until liquid begins to bubble.

Spoon out 3 tablespoons of liquid and dissolve cornstarch in this liquid. Slowly stir mixture back into skillet. Reduce heat, place biscuits on top, cover, and simmer for 5 minutes. Turn off burner and allow to sit for 5 minutes.

ESTIMATED PREPARATION TIME: 5 minutes.

ESTIMATED COOKING TIME: 10 minutes + 5 minutes
sitting time.

189 Calories
14.0 g Protein
23.1 g Carbohydrates
4.3 g Fat
0.7 g Fiber
1012 mg Sodium
32 mg Cholesterol

Quick Macaroni and Cheese

Yield: 4 servings

Cook macaroni in boiling water for 7 minutes, drain, and rinse. Place cooked macaroni in a microwavable medium glass bowl or casserole. Pour milk over macaroni, then tear cheese slices and sprinkle over macaroni. Cover and microwave on High for 3 minutes. Stir and serve with salad and rolls.

1 cup uncooked elbow
    macaroni
1 quart boiling water
½ cup skim milk
3 slices reduced-fat
    American cheese

ESTIMATED PREPARATION TIME: 5 minutes.

ESTIMATED COOKING TIME: 10 minutes.

147 Calories
7.4 g Protein
22.9 g Carbohydrates
2.8 g Fat
1.1 g Fiber
264 mg Sodium
8 mg Cholesterol

Hot Dog Kabobs

Yield: 6 servings

1 package (16 ounces)
   fat-free wieners cut
   into bite-size pieces
1 pound cherry tomatoes,
   stems removed
1 can (8⅕ ounces)
   pineapple chunks,
   drained
3 sweet pickles, cut into
   ½-inch chunks
½ cup reduced-fat
   Catalina-style dressing

Alternate wiener pieces, tomatoes, pineapple, and pickle chunks on wooden or metal skewers.

Place skewers on a broiling rack that has been lightly coated with cooking oil spray. Brush with the dressing. Turn on oven broiler (500 degrees) and broil kabobs on center rack of oven for 3 minutes. Turn, brush with dressing, and broil for an additional 2 minutes.

Note: Serve with crackers and fruit.

ESTIMATED PREPARATION TIME: 15 minutes.

ESTIMATED COOKING TIME: 5 minutes.

144 Calories
8.3 g Protein
20.1 g Carbohydrates
0.3 g Fat
1.4 g Fiber
1241 mg Sodium
0 mg Cholesterol

Cracker Pizza

Yield: 4 servings

Preheat oven to 375 degrees.

In a small bowl, mix tomato paste and seasoning until well blended. Place crackers on a nonstick cookie sheet, and place 1 teaspoon of tomato paste on each cracker, spreading evenly. Lightly sprinkle cheeses onto crackers. Top with salami, pepperoni, vegetables, etc. as desired.

Bake for 8 to 10 minutes, or until cheese has melted.

ESTIMATED PREPARATION TIME: 5 minutes.

ESTIMATED COOKING TIME: 8 minutes.

¼ cup tomato paste
½ teaspoon Italian seasoning
8 medium Rye Krisp (or similar) crackers
¾ cup reduced-fat shredded Cheddar cheese
¾ cup reduced-fat shredded mozzarella cheese
additional toppings as desired

160 Calories
15.1 g Protein
15.7 g Carbohydrates
6.4 g Fat
4.3 g Fiber
400 mg Sodium
20 mg Cholesterol

Quick Straw-and-Hay

Yield: 8 servings

¼ pound uncooked plain
    fettuccine
¼ pound uncooked
    spinach fettuccine
½ cup frozen peas
¼ cup prepared bacon bits
1 tub (10 ounces)
    prepared 'lite'
    Alfredo sauce
½ cup reduced-fat
    shredded Parmesan
    cheese

Prepare pasta according to package directions, drain, and rinse. Place cooked pasta in a large microwavable bowl; add peas, bacon bits, and Alfredo sauce, and toss.

Microwave on Medium High for 10 minutes, and toss again. Sprinkle with Parmesan cheese and serve.

ESTIMATED PREPARATION TIME: 15 minutes.

ESTIMATED COOKING TIME: 10 minutes.

181 Calories
7.8 g Protein
22.3 g Carbohydrates
6.2 g Fat
1.4 g Fiber
299 mg Sodium
27 mg Cholesterol

Busy Mom's Lowfat Cookbook

Chapter 3

A+ After-School Snacks

Every weekday afternoon, in homes across North America, front doors fly open and miniature whirlwinds blow in asking, "Can I have a snack?" Advertisers know this. Grocers know this. We're virtually bombarded with clever commercials, brightly colored packaging, and an overwhelming variety of cookies, candies, snack cakes, chips, and microwave popcorn. At last count, my local grocer had three aisles devoted to snack foods—which didn't include the aisle of soft drinks or the bakery department!

The truth is, we love to snack. We love to nibble salty, crunchy snacks, and sweet, gooey treats. Eating healthy snacks often isn't as appealing as breaking into a new bag of nacho-flavored corn chips or a box of chocolate-covered chocolate cupcakes.

Your children might pass up that bag of chips in favor of one of these snacks, and they won't even know that the treat they're eating is more nutritious!

After-School Oatmeal Cookies

Yield: 3 dozen cookies

Preheat oven to 375 degrees. In a large bowl, cream together sugar, yogurt, margarine, sweet potatoes, and vanilla. In a separate bowl, combine oats, flour, baking soda, and salt. Add to the creamed mixture and mix well. Dough should be stiff.

Roll teaspoonfuls of dough into small balls. Place on a nonstick cookie sheet about 3 inches apart. Press each cookie with the bottom of a drinking glass that has been dipped in water. Bake for 8 to 10 minutes, or until golden brown.

¾ cup packed brown
    sugar
½ cup nonfat plain yogurt
2 tablespoons reduced-fat
    margarine, softened
1 jar (4 ounces) puréed
    sweet potatoes
1 teaspoon vanilla extract
2 cups quick-cooking oats
1 cup whole wheat flour
1 teaspoon baking soda
½ teaspoon salt

ESTIMATED PREPARATION TIME: 15 minutes.

ESTIMATED COOKING TIME: 16 to 24 minutes.

HIGH ALTITUDE NOTE: Increase oven temperature to
400 degrees.

55 Calories
1.4 g Protein
10.9 g Carbohydrates
0.7 g Fat
1.0 g Fiber
76 mg Sodium
0 mg Cholesterol

After-School Molasses Cookies

Yield: 3 dozen cookies

2 cups flour
2 teaspoons cinnamon
1 teaspoon ginger
1 teaspoon baking soda
½ teaspoon salt
1 jar (4 ounces) puréed
    prunes (baby food)
1 cup sugar, plus ½ cup
    for coating
¼ cup canola oil
¼ cup unsulfured molasses
2 large egg whites, lightly
    beaten

Preheat oven to 350 degrees. Place flour, cinnamon, ginger, baking soda, and salt in a large mixing bowl, and stir to combine. In a smaller bowl, mix together prune purée, sugar, oil, and molasses. Add to the dry ingredients, add the egg whites, and stir until just combined.

Place some additional sugar (about ½ cup) in a cereal bowl. Spoon dough by the teaspoonful and shape into balls. Roll the balls through the sugar and place on a nonstick cookie sheet about 3 inches apart. Gently press, using waxed paper and the bottom of a drinking glass. Bake for 8 to 10 minutes.

ESTIMATED PREPARATION TIME: 15 minutes.

ESTIMATED COOKING TIME: 16 to 24 minutes.

79 Calories
1.0 g Protein
15.6 g Carbohydrates
1.6 g Fat
0.3 g Fiber
69 mg Sodium
0 mg Cholesterol

After-School Raisin Cookies

Yield: 3 dozen cookies

Preheat oven to 375 degrees. Place margarine, cream cheese, sugar, and egg in a large mixing bowl and cream together. Stir in applesauce. In a smaller bowl, combine flour, baking soda, salt, and cinnamon, then add to cream cheese mixture. Stir until well blended. Fold in the raisins and pecans.

Drop dough by teaspoonful, about 2 inches apart, onto a nonstick cookie sheet and bake for 10 to 12 minutes.

ESTIMATED PREPARATION TIME: 10 minutes.

ESTIMATED COOKING TIME: 30 to 36 minutes.

HIGH ALTITUDE NOTE: Increase oven temperature to 400 degrees.

¼ cup reduced-fat margarine, softened
¼ cup reduced-fat cream cheese, softened
¾ cup lightly packed brown sugar
1 egg
½ cup applesauce
2 cups flour
½ teaspoon baking soda
½ teaspoon salt
½ teaspoon cinnamon
1 cup raisins
½ cup chopped pecans

82 Calories
1.4 g Protein
14.5 g Carbohydrates
2.3 g Fat
0.6 g Fiber
70 mg Sodium
7 mg Cholesterol

After-School Banana Bars

Yield: 42 bars

¼ cup reduced-fat
    margarine, softened
¾ cup sugar
¼ cup egg substitute
2 bananas, mashed
1 teaspoon vanilla
2 cups flour
2 teaspoons baking
    powder
½ teaspoon salt
½ cup chopped walnuts

Preheat oven to 375 degrees. Place margarine, sugar, egg substitute, and mashed banana in a large mixing bowl and cream together. Stir in vanilla. Add flour, baking powder, and salt, then mix well. Fold in nuts. Spread dough on a nonstick cookie sheet that has been lightly coated with a cooking oil spray.

Bake for 15 to 20 minutes. Cool and cut into bars.

ESTIMATED PREPARATION TIME: 10 minutes.

ESTIMATED COOKING TIME: 15 minutes.

56 Calories
1.0 g Protein
9.9 g Carbohydrates
1.5 g Fat
0.3 g Fiber
57 mg Sodium
0 mg Cholesterol

Easy Granola Bars

Yield: 9 bars

Place margarine and marshmallows in a large micro-wavable bowl, and microwave on High for 1 minute. Turn bowl and microwave on High for an additional 30 seconds. Add granola, raisins, and nuts, stirring to coat well.

   Press into a 9-inch square baking pan that has been lightly coated with cooking oil spray. Chill for half an hour or more, and cut.

¼ cup reduced-fat margarine
1 cup marshmallows
2 cups lowfat granola
½ cup raisins
½ cup chopped pecans

ESTIMATED PREPARATION TIME: 5 minutes plus chilling time.

ESTIMATED COOKING TIME: 1½ minutes.

221 Calories
3.3 g Protein
36.9 g Carbohydrates
8.1 g Fat
2.6 g Fiber
116 mg Sodium
0 mg Cholesterol

Chewy Pumpkin Bars

Yield: 32 bars

1 cup flour
½ cup sugar
1 teaspoon baking soda
½ teaspoon cinnamon
⅓ teaspoon nutmeg
⅛ teaspoon ginger
½ teaspoon salt
2 tablespoons canola oil
1 cup canned pumpkin
½ cup raisins

Cream Cheese Frosting
¼ cup fat-free cream
   cheese, softened
1 cup powdered sugar

Preheat oven to 375 degrees. Place flour, sugar, baking soda, cinnamon, nutmeg, ginger, salt, oil, and pumpkin in a large bowl and mix well. Batter will be slightly lumpy. Fold in raisins.

Lightly coat a 13- × 9-inch baking pan with cooking oil spray, and spread dough into pan. Bake for 20 minutes. Allow to cool, frost if desired (recipe below), and cut into 1- × 3-inch bars.

For Cream Cheese Frosting: Place ingredients in a small bowl and mix well.

ESTIMATED PREPARATION TIME: 5 minutes.

ESTIMATED COOKING TIME: 20 minutes.

ESTIMATED PREPARATION TIME: 2 minutes for frosting.

Pumpkin Bars
44 Calories
0.6 g Protein
8.8 g Carbohydrates
0.9 g Fat
0.4 g Fiber
68 mg Sodium
0 mg Cholesterol

Cream Cheese Frosting
14 Calories
0.2 g Protein
3.2 g Carbohydrates
0 g Fat
0 g Fiber
10 mg Sodium
0 mg Cholesterol

Peach Crisp

Yield: 32 bars

Preheat oven to 425 degrees. Place oats, wheat germ, flour, sugar, cinnamon, and salt in a large bowl and stir. Drizzle oil over mixture and stir with a fork to combine. Reserve ½ cup of the mixture to use as a topping.

Lightly coat a 13- × 9-inch baking pan with cooking oil spray, and spread mixture evenly in bottom. Drain ¼ cup of liquid from canned peaches, and purée remaining contents of can in blender or food processor. Pour puréed peaches slowly and evenly over mixture in baking pan, then sprinkle reserved mixture evenly on top.

Bake for 20 minutes. Allow to cool thoroughly before slicing into 1- × 3-inch bars.

2 cups quick-cooking oats
½ cup wheat germ
¼ cup flour
½ cup packed brown sugar
½ teaspoon cinnamon
½ teaspoon salt
2 tablespoons canola oil
1 can (20 ounces) diced peaches, in juice

ESTIMATED PREPARATION TIME: 15 minutes.

ESTIMATED COOKING TIME: 20 minutes.

58 Calories
1.4 g Protein
10.6 g Carbohydrates
1.4 g Fat
1.1 g Fiber
36 mg Sodium
0 mg Cholesterol

Rocky Road Pudding Cup

Yield: 8 servings

1 package (3½ ounces)
   fat-free instant
   chocolate pudding
   mix
2 cups skim milk
1½ cups miniature
   marshmallows
½ cup chopped dry
   roasted peanuts

Prepare pudding according to package directions, using 2 cups of milk. Fold in marshmallows and nuts. Spoon mixture into individual plastic cups and chill.

ESTIMATED PREPARATION TIME: 10 minutes.

142 Calories
4.0 g Protein
24.3 g Carbohydrates
3.6 g Fat
0.6 g Fiber
299 mg Sodium
1 mg Cholesterol

Busy Mom's Lowfat Cookbook

Lemon Berry Cups

Yield: 8 servings

Blend the yogurt and whipped topping together in a mixing bowl, then fold in the berries. Spoon mixture into individual plastic cups and chill.

1 cup nonfat lemon yogurt
1 cup reduced-fat
    whipped topping
2 cups fresh berries

ESTIMATED PREPARATION TIME: 5 minutes.

52 Calories
1.5 g Protein
9.0 g Carbohydrates
2.2 g Fat
1.5 g Fiber
23 mg Sodium
1 mg Cholesterol

Mini Snack Kabobs

Yield: 4 servings

½ pound fresh
    strawberries
½ pound seedless white
    grapes
4 ounces reduced-fat
    Cheddar cheese,
    cubed

Using toothpicks as skewers, assemble mini-kabobs by sliding one grape, one cube of cheese, and one slice of strawberry onto each toothpick.

ESTIMATED PREPARATION TIME: 5 minutes.

138 Calories
8.7 g Protein
15.1 g Carbohydrates
5.5 g Fat
1.9 g Fiber
212 mg Sodium
20 mg Cholesterol

Busy Mom's Lowfat Cookbook

Vegetables with Cream Cheese Dip

Yield: 4 servings

Arrange vegetables on a large plate. In a small bowl, cream together softened cream cheese, lemon juice, and seasonings.

ESTIMATED PREPARATION TIME: 5 minutes.

1 package (8 ounces) carrot sticks
1 package (8 ounces) celery sticks
1 cup fresh cauliflower florets
½ cup fat-free cream cheese, softened
2 tablespoons lemon juice
¼ teaspoon garlic powder
½ teaspoon Mrs. Dash brand seasoning

67 Calories
5.6 g Protein
10.8 g Carbohydrates
0.2 g Fat
3.3 g Fiber
243 mg Sodium
5 mg Cholesterol

Quick Toasted Cereal Snack Mix

Yield: 10 servings

1 cup Cheerios brand
   cereal
1 cup Crispix brand
   cereal
1 cup Wheat Chex brand
   cereal
1 cup pretzel nuggets
1 cup unsalted dry-
   roasted peanuts
   Seasoned salt

Preheat oven to 400 degrees. Mix cereals, pretzels, and peanuts in a 13- × 9-inch baking pan and spread evenly. Lightly coat cereal mixture with a cooking oil spray, then sprinkle with seasoned salt. Toast in oven for 5 minutes, stir, and toast for an additional 5 minutes. Allow to cool before serving.

ESTIMATED PREPARATION TIME: 5 minutes.

ESTIMATED COOKING TIME: 10 minutes.

141 Calories
4.5 g Protein
17.8 g Carbohydrates
6.4 g Fat
2.0 g Fiber
220 mg Sodium
0 mg Cholesterol

Homemade Tortilla Chips

Yield: 8 servings

Preheat oven to 400 degrees. Using a sharp knife, quarter tortillas and arrange quarters side by side on a non-stick cookie sheet. Lightly coat tortilla quarters with cooking oil spray, and then salt lightly.

Bake for 8 to 10 minutes, remove, and allow to cool. Repeat until all tortillas are baked.

Note: These chips are lower in fat and salt than ordinary tortilla chips.

1 package (11½ ounces) corn tortillas
salt to taste

ESTIMATED PREPARATION TIME: 5 minutes.

ESTIMATED COOKING TIME: 16 to 24 minutes.

91 Calories
2.0 g Protein
18.4 g Carbohydrates
0.8 g Fat
2.1 g Fiber
72 mg Sodium
0 mg Cholesterol

Nacho Popcorn

Yield: 4 servings

4 cups hot-air-popped
popcorn
1 teaspoon chili powder
1 teaspoon garlic salt
1 teaspoon paprika
½ teaspoon pepper

Place popcorn in a large clean paper bag. Stir seasonings together in a small bowl, then sprinkle over popcorn. Fold top of bag to seal and shake vigorously to evenly coat popcorn. Pour popcorn into serving bowl.

ESTIMATED PREPARATION TIME: 5 minutes.

35 Calories
1.0 g Protein
7.1 g Carbohydrates
0.7 g Fat
0.7 g Fiber
520 mg Sodium
0 mg Cholesterol

Quick Caramel Corn

Yield: 4 servings

Place popcorn in a large serving bowl. Place remaining ingredients in a small nonstick saucepan. Bring to a boil over medium heat, stirring constantly, until sauce begins to bubble. Drizzle over popcorn and toss to coat evenly.

4 cups hot-air-popped popcorn
¼ cup reduced-fat margarine
¼ cup brown sugar
½ teaspoon salt

ESTIMATED PREPARATION TIME: 5 minutes.

ESTIMATED COOKING TIME: 3 minutes.

135 Calories
0.8 g Protein
20.0 g Carbohydrates
6.2 g Fat
0.4 g Fiber
411 mg Sodium
0 mg Cholesterol

Quesadilla Snacks

Yield: 4 servings

8 flour tortillas
1 cup reduced-fat
    shredded Cheddar
    cheese
½ cup reduced-fat
    shredded jack cheese
¼ cup diced jalapeño
    chilies

Preheat nonstick griddle over medium heat. Lay one tortilla on the hot griddle and sprinkle with ¼ cup of Cheddar cheese and 2 tablespoons of jack cheese. Sprinkle 1 tablespoon of peppers over the cheeses and place another tortilla on top. Cook for 2 minutes and carefully turn. Cook for an additional 2 minutes and set aside.

Repeat until all ingredients have been used. Slice the quesadillas into quarters and serve with salsa if desired.

ESTIMATED PREPARATION TIME: 2 minutes.

ESTIMATED COOKING TIME: 20 minutes.

312 Calories
16.7 g Protein
36.5 g Carbohydrates
11.2 g Fat
1.9 g Fiber
535 mg Sodium
30 mg Cholesterol

Hot Pretzels

Yield: 6 large pretzels

Preheat oven to 450 degrees. Dissolve yeast and sugar in warm water in a large mixing bowl. Add ½ cup of flour and beat until smooth. Gradually add remaining flour and salt, mixing until a soft dough forms.

Transfer dough to a lightly floured work area and knead gently for 5 minutes. Pull off dough by the handful and roll into a long snake-like strip. Arrange on non-stick cookie sheet in pretzel shape. Sprinkle with additional salt if desired.

Allow to rise for 15 to 20 minutes. Bake for 10 minutes or until golden brown. Serve with prepared mustard.

1 package fast-rising yeast
1 teaspoon sugar
⅓ cup warm water
2 cups flour
½ teaspoon salt

ESTIMATED PREPARATION TIME: 20 minutes plus rising time (15–20 minutes).

ESTIMATED COOKING TIME: 10 minutes.

156 Calories
4.7 g Protein
32.6 g Carbohydrates
0.4 g Fat
1.1 g Fiber
179 mg Sodium
0 mg Cholesterol

Lemon Yogurt Pops

Yield: 6 to 8 pops

1½ cups lemon-flavored, fat-free aspartame-sweetened yogurt
½ cup frozen lemonade concentrate, thawed
3 tablespoons honey (or 1 tablespoon plus 1 teaspoon powdered sugar)

Place yogurt, lemonade concentrate, and honey in a blender, and pulse on low speed until well combined. Pour into paper drinking cups. Place cups in the freezer for 30 minutes, then place a popsicle stick in the center of each cup. Freeze for another hour.

ESTIMATED PREPARATION TIME: 5 minutes plus 1½ hours freezing time.

81 Calories
1.8 g Protein
18.9 g Carbohydrates
0.1 g Fat
0 g Fiber
28 mg Sodium
1 mg Cholesterol

Busy Mom's Lowfat Cookbook

Strawberry Yogurt Pops

Yield: 6 to 8 pops

Place strawberries in a small microwavable glass bowl. Sprinkle with sugar and microwave on High for 2 minutes. Pour into blender or food processor and purée. Add yogurt and pulse until combined. Pour into paper cups. Place cups in the freezer for 30 minutes, then place popsicle sticks in the center of each cup. Freeze for another hour.

1 cup fresh strawberries
¼ cup sugar
1 cup nonfat strawberry
   yogurt

ESTIMATED PREPARATION TIME: 5 minutes plus 1½ hours freezing time.

44 Calories
1.3 g Protein
9.7 g Carbohydrates
0.1 g Fat
0.5 g Fiber
19 mg Sodium
1 mg Cholesterol

More Quick Snacks

- Reduced-fat wheat crackers with fat-free cream cheese and a strawberry half as garnish.
- Reduced-fat wheat crackers with small slices of reduced-fat cheese and seedless red grape halves as garnish.
- Rice cakes topped with reduced-fat peanut butter and chopped raisins.
- Celery stalks filled with reduced-fat cream cheese and crushed pineapple.
- 2 tablespoons nonfat cottage cheese on a peach half.
- Fruit salad from any combination of fresh fruits in season, or canned fruit cocktail in juice with dried, chopped fruits added.
- ½ cup salad shrimp served with ½ tablespoon cocktail sauce.
- Biscuits, split and filled with thin-sliced lean ham and cheese.

Chapter 4

Soup's On!

Quick Vegetable Soup	Quick Chicken Rice Soup
Quick Creamy Vegetable Soup	Quick Chicken Noodle Soup
Quick Pumpkin Vegetable Soup	Quick Clam Chowder
Quick Cream of Broccoli Soup	Quick Chili
Quick Pea Soup	Gazpacho
Quick Swedish Pea Soup	Harvest Tortellini Soup
Quick Tomato Soup	Winter Fruit Soup
Quick Potato Soup	Blueberry Soup
Quick Sweet Potato Soup	Cheery Cherry Soup
	Cool Apricot Soup
	Cool Cantaloupe Soup

I love soup. It's the ultimate in "comfort food"—especially on those fateful nights when I realize that, once again, I forgot to thaw something for dinner. Soup is simple. Soup is good for you. It fills your home with delicious aromas, and your tummy with warm nourishment.

My children, on the other hand, don't always share my enthusiasm for soup: "Are there onions in this? I don't like onions!"

Some adult tastes aren't popular with younger palates. You won't find my recipe for Cream of Asparagus Soup in this cookbook. You *will* find recipes for some delightful and surprising concoctions, including cool, fruity soups for hot summer nights. You'll also find fast, easy recipes for old-fashioned favorites.

To round out a well-balanced meal, serve these soups with fresh breads and salads.

Quick Vegetable Soup

Yield: 4 servings

Place all ingredients in a small pot, and bring to a low boil over medium-low heat.

ESTIMATED PREPARATION TIME: 2 minutes.

ESTIMATED COOKING TIME: 5 minutes.

1 can (15 ounces) crushed tomatoes
1 cup water
1 teaspoon beef bouillon granules (or 1 cube)
1 cup leftover vegetables
2 teaspoons parsley flakes

51 Calories
2.5 g Protein
10.9 g Carbohydrates
0.4 g Fat
2.2 g Fiber
417 mg Sodium
0 mg Cholesterol

Quick Creamy Vegetable Soup

Yield: 4 servings

1 can (15¾ ounces)
   cream of mushroom
   soup
2 cups water
1 package (10 ounces)
   frozen mixed
   vegetables, thawed
½ teaspoon Mrs. Dash
   brand seasoning

Place all ingredients in a small pot, and bring to a low boil over medium-low heat. Simmer on low heat until vegetables are tender, stirring occasionally.

ESTIMATED PREPARATION TIME: 2 minutes.

ESTIMATED COOKING TIME: 10 minutes.

169 Calories
5.6 g Protein
25.7 g Carbohydrates
6.0 g Fat
6.0 g Fiber
675 mg Sodium
1 mg Cholesterol

Busy Mom's Lowfat Cookbook

Quick Pumpkin Vegetable Soup

Yield: 4 servings

Place all ingredients in a small pot and bring to a low boil over medium-low heat, stirring frequently. Simmer on low heat until vegetables are tender, stirring occasionally.

ESTIMATED PREPARATION TIME: 2 minutes.

ESTIMATED COOKING TIME: 10 minutes.

1 can (15 ounces) pumpkin
2 cups water
½ cup finely chopped onion
1 package (10 ounces) frozen mixed vegetables, thawed
⅛ teaspoon curry powder
⅛ teaspoon cinnamon

120 Calories
5.3 g Protein
26.7 g Carbohydrates
0.5 g Fat
7.1 g Fiber
60 mg Sodium
0 mg Cholesterol

Quick Cream of Broccoli Soup

Yield: 4 servings

1 can (15¾ ounces)
    cream of mushroom
    soup
2 cups water
1 package (10 ounces)
    frozen chopped
    broccoli, thawed
dash of pepper

Place all ingredients in a small pot, and bring to a low boil over medium-low heat, stirring occasionally. Simmer on low heat, stirring frequently until broccoli is tender.

ESTIMATED PREPARATION TIME: 2 minutes.

ESTIMATED COOKING TIME: 10 minutes.

119 Calories
5.8 g Protein
13.5 g Carbohydrates
5.9 g Fat
4.0 g Fiber
656 mg Sodium
1 mg Cholesterol

Busy Mom's Lowfat Cookbook

Quick Pea Soup

Yield: 4 servings

Purée entire contents of canned peas in blender or food processor. Place all ingredients in a small pot, and bring to a low boil over medium-low heat, stirring frequently to prevent scorching.

1 can (16 ounces) peas
1 cup water
1 teaspoon chicken
    bouillon granules
    (or 1 cube)
dash of pepper

ESTIMATED PREPARATION TIME: 2 minutes.

ESTIMATED COOKING TIME: 5 minutes.

62 Calories
3.9 g Protein
11.0 g Carbohydrates
0.3 g Fat
2.9 g Fiber
610 mg Sodium
0 mg Cholesterol

Quick Swedish Pea Soup

Yield: 4 servings

1 can (16 ounces) peas
1 cup water
1 teaspoon beef bouillon
 granules (or 1 cube)
⅛ teaspoon ginger
½ cup diced ham
1 teaspoon sugar

Purée entire contents of canned peas in blender or food processor. Place all ingredients in a small pot, and bring to a low boil over medium-low heat, stirring frequently to prevent scorching.

ESTIMATED PREPARATION TIME: 2 minutes.

ESTIMATED COOKING TIME: 5 minutes.

90 Calories
7.7 g Protein
11.8 g Carbohydrates
1.3 g Fat
2.9 g Fiber
753 mg Sodium
9 mg Cholesterol

Busy Mom's Lowfat Cookbook

Quick Tomato Soup

Yield: 4 servings

Stir tomatoes, water, cinnamon, and onion together and bring to a low boil over medium-low heat, stirring occasionally. Turn off burner and allow to cool for 2 minutes. Slowly stir in evaporated milk.

1 can (15 ounces) crushed
   tomatoes
1 cup water
¼ teaspoon cinnamon
1 teaspoon dehydrated
   minced onion
1 can (12 ounces)
   evaporated milk

ESTIMATED PREPARATION TIME: 2 minutes.

ESTIMATED COOKING TIME: 7 minutes.

144 Calories
7.2 g Protein
14.3 g Carbohydrates
7.1 g Fat
0.6 g Fiber
291 mg Sodium
26 mg Cholesterol

Quick Potato Soup

Yield: 4 servings

4 cups water
2 teaspoons chicken
    bouillon granules (or
    2 cubes)
1½ cups leftover mashed
    potatoes
1 teaspoon dehydrated
    minced onion
¼ teaspoon celery seed
⅛ teaspoon pepper

Place all ingredients in a small pot and bring to a low boil over medium-low heat, stirring occasionally.

ESTIMATED PREPARATION TIME: 2 minutes.

ESTIMATED COOKING TIME: 5 minutes.

VARIATION: Add ½ cup cooked rice or reduced-fat shredded cheese.

67 Calories
1.9 g Protein
14.7 g Carbohydrates
0.6 g Fat
0.3 g Fiber
818 mg Sodium
2 mg Cholesterol

Busy Mom's Lowfat Cookbook

Quick Sweet Potato Soup

Yield: 4 servings

Purée entire contents of canned yams in blender or food processor. Place all ingredients in a small pot, and bring to a low boil over medium-low heat, stirring frequently.

Estimated preparation time: 2 minutes.

Estimated cooking time: 5 minutes.

1 can (16 ounces) yams in light syrup
2 cups water
2 teaspoons chicken bouillon granules (or 2 cubes)
¼ teaspoon cinnamon
¼ teaspoon nutmeg

118 Calories
0.4 g Protein
28.0 g Carbohydrates
0.5 g Fat
2.1 g Fiber
604 mg Sodium
1 mg Cholesterol

Quick Chicken Rice Soup

Yield: 4 servings

½ cup uncooked Minute
   rice
4 cups water
3 teaspoons chicken
   bouillon granules
   (or 3 cubes)
½ cup diced leftover
   chicken meat
⅛ teaspoon curry powder
½ cup leftover vegetables
   (if desired)

Place all ingredients in a small pot and bring to a low boil over medium-low heat, stirring occasionally.

ESTIMATED PREPARATION TIME: 5 minutes.

ESTIMATED COOKING TIME: 5 minutes.

99 Calories
6.9 g Protein
14.3 g Carbohydrates
1.4 g Fat
1.0 g Fiber
892 mg Sodium
15 mg Cholesterol

Busy Mom's Lowfat Cookbook

Quick Chicken Noodle Soup

Yield: 4 servings

Place all ingredients in a small pot and bring to a low boil over medium-low heat. Cook until noodles are tender, stirring occasionally.

ESTIMATED PREPARATION TIME: 5 minutes.

ESTIMATED COOKING TIME: 10 minutes.

½ cup uncooked noodles
4 cups water
3 teaspoons chicken bouillon granules (or 3 cubes)
½ cup diced leftover chicken meat
½ teaspoon parsley flakes
½ cup leftover vegetables (if desired)

103 Calories
7.7 g Protein
14.1 g Carbohydrates
1.6 g Fat
1.3 g Fiber
893 mg Sodium
15 mg Cholesterol

Quick Clam Chowder

Yield: 4 servings

1 can (5 ounces) minced
    clams, drained
1 celery stalk, diced
1 carrot, diced
4 cups water
2 teaspoons chicken
    bouillon granules
    (or 2 cubes)
1 cup leftover mashed
    potatoes
1 teaspoon minced onion
¼ teaspoon pepper

Place all ingredients in a small pot and bring to a low boil over medium-low heat. Cook until vegetables are tender, stirring frequently.

ESTIMATED PREPARATION TIME: 5 minutes.

ESTIMATED COOKING TIME: 10 minutes.

90 Calories
7.6 g Protein
14.1 g Carbohydrates
1.0 g Fat
0.9 g Fiber
1077 mg Sodium
20 mg Cholesterol

Quick Chili

Yield: 4 servings

Place all ingredients in a medium pot and bring to a low boil over medium-low heat, stirring frequently.

ESTIMATED PREPARATION TIME: 2 minutes.

ESTIMATED COOKING TIME: 5 minutes.

1 can (15 ounces) diced tomatoes
1 can (6 ounces) tomato paste
2 cups water
1 can (15 ounces) kidney beans, drained
1 can (15 ounces) black beans, drained and rinsed
¼ teaspoon chili powder
½ teaspoon dehydrated minced onion
⅛ teaspoon pepper

227 Calories
13.5 g Protein
43.8 g Carbohydrates
1.3 g Fat
10.9 g Fiber
1156 mg Sodium
0 mg Cholesterol

Gazpacho

Yield: 4 servings

2 cans (15 ounces each)
    diced tomatoes
1 cup diced zucchini
1 cup chopped green bell
    pepper
½ cup chopped onion
¼ cup red wine vinegar
2 tablespoons olive oil
1 tablespoon minced
    garlic
    hot pepper sauce

Place half of the tomatoes, zucchini, bell pepper, and onion in a blender and purée. Add vinegar, olive oil, garlic, and hot pepper sauce and pulse blender until combined. Stir in remaining vegetables, cover, and chill.

ESTIMATED PREPARATION TIME: 15 minutes.

131 Calories
3.2 g Protein
16.4 g Carbohydrates
7.5 g Fat
2.4 g Fiber
369 mg Sodium
0 mg Cholesterol

Busy Mom's Lowfat Cookbook

Harvest Tortellini Soup

Yield: 4 to 6 hearty servings

Place all ingredients (except tortellini) in a small pot and bring to a boil over medium-low heat. Reduce heat, stir in tortellini, and cover. Simmer for 10 minutes, stirring occasionally to keep tortellini from sticking.

ESTIMATED PREPARATION TIME: 5 minutes.

ESTIMATED COOKING TIME: 15 minutes.

1 can (15 ounces) diced tomatoes
4 cups water
2 teaspoons beef bouillon granules (or 2 cubes)
1 teaspoon minced garlic
1 teaspoon Italian seasonings
1 tablespoon olive oil
1 package (12 ounces) frozen Italian mixed vegetables, thawed
1 package (9 ounces) cheese tortellini

187 Calories
8.7 g Protein
26.4 g Carbohydrates
6.1 g Fat
2.5 g Fiber
525 mg Sodium
49 mg Cholesterol

Winter Fruit Soup

Yield: 4 servings

1 cup frozen pineapple
    juice concentrate,
    thawed

3 cups water

1 cup prepared orange
    juice

2 cups mixed dried fruits,
    diced

½ cup raisins

¼ teaspoon cinnamon

¼ teaspoon ginger

Place pineapple juice concentrate, water, and orange juice in a large saucepan. Add remaining ingredients. Bring to a boil over medium-low heat. Cover, reduce heat, and simmer for 20 minutes, stirring occasionally. Serve hot or cold.

ESTIMATED PREPARATION TIME: 5 minutes.

ESTIMATED COOKING TIME: 25 minutes.

359 Calories
3.5 g Protein
91.8 g Carbohydrates
0.5 g Fat
3.1 g Fiber
21 mg Sodium
0 mg Cholesterol

Blueberry Soup

Yield: 4 servings

Place all ingredients in a medium saucepan and heat, stirring gently, until soup begins to bubble and blueberries are cooked. Serve with a dollop of nonfat plain yogurt, if desired.

ESTIMATED PREPARATION TIME: 2 minutes.

ESTIMATED COOKING TIME: 12 minutes.

2 cups water
1 cup prepared orange juice
2 cups fresh or frozen blueberries, thawed
¼ cup sugar
1 tablespoon corn starch
¼ teaspoon cinnamon

122 Calories
0.9 g Protein
30.8 g Carbohydrates
0.3 g Fat
1.8 g Fiber
9 mg Sodium
0 mg Cholesterol

Cheery Cherry Soup

Yield: 4 servings

1 can (16 ounces) "lite"
   aspartame-sweetened
   cherry pie filling
2 cups apple juice
⅛ teaspoon cinnamon
¼ cup dry white wine

Place all ingredients in a medium saucepan. Heat on low, stirring gently, until soup begins to bubble. Serve hot or cold. Garnish with a dollop of whipped cream or lowfat plain yogurt, if desired.

ESTIMATED PREPARATION TIME: 2 minutes.

ESTIMATED COOKING TIME: 5 minutes.

164 Calories
0.1 g Protein
38.7 g Carbohydrates
0.2 g Fat
0.1 g Fiber
31 mg Sodium
0 mg Cholesterol

Busy Mom's Lowfat Cookbook

Cool Apricot Soup

Yield: 4 servings

Purée entire contents of canned apricots in a blender or food processor. Stir in milk and yogurt. Chill.

1 can (28 ounces) apricots in juice
1 cup skim milk
½ cup nonfat plain yogurt

ESTIMATED PREPARATION TIME: 5 minutes.

131 Calories
5.0 g Protein
29.4 g Carbohydrates
0.2 g Fat
0.7 g Fiber
61 mg Sodium
2 mg Cholesterol

Cool Cantaloupe Soup

Yield: 4 servings

3 small ripe cantaloupes,
   seeded and cut up
2 cups prepared orange
   juice
¼ cup sugar
¼ cup dry white wine

Purée all ingredients in a blender or food processor. Serve chilled. Garnish with a dollop of whipped cream or lowfat plain yogurt, if desired.

ESTIMATED PREPARATION TIME: **10 minutes.**

252 Calories
4.4 g Protein
58.9 g Carbohydrates
1.2 g Fat
3.5 g Fiber
37 mg Sodium
0 mg Cholesterol

Chapter 5

For Kids Who Hate Veggies

Vegetables with Honey
Yogurt Dip

Easy Skewered
Vegetables

Cauliflower Citrus Salad

Quick Cabbage Patch
Salad

Easy Carrot Raisin Salad

Farmer John's Salad

Fusilli Fruit and
Vegetable Salad

Simply Potato Salad

Kid-Pleasing Waldorf
Salad

Italian Broccoli

Florida Citrus Broccoli

Corny Confetti

Spicy Polynesian Carrots

Southern-Style Green
Beans

Quick Snow Peas and
Carrots

Minty Peas

Sweet and Creamy
Potatoes

Sesame Spinach

Quick Stuffed Tomatoes

Golden Zucchini Sticks

Rare is the parent gifted with a child who loves vegetables. My mother was lucky; I preferred brussels sprouts to chocolate pudding. I begged for spinach and broccoli—so often, in fact, that I'm amazed my siblings speak to me. Yet when I had children, I joined the ranks of parents who launch into a victory dance when Junior manages to swallow a few green beans.

Then the "five a day" cry resounded across the country. Five? A day? Talk about Mission Impossible!

When bribing, cajoling, and "guilting" my children into eating their vegetables failed, I sought the advice of seasoned veterans in the vegetable wars. Along the way, I discovered tips, tricks, and sneaky strategies.

For example, kids love amusing shapes, colors, and textures. If the concept of vegetables as art seems absurd, wait until you see some of these colorful dishes. Children also love sweet tastes. Several of these recipes appeal to little sweet-tooths, without a great deal of sugar added.

I've discovered that "five a day" isn't as impossible as it sounds. You just need to play with your food!

Vegetables with Honey Yogurt Dip

Yield: Serves up to 8 people

Place yogurt, cream cheese, and honey in a blender and pulse until smooth and creamy. Pour into a small bowl and chill.

Arrange vegetables on a large serving dish. Place the chilled dip in the center of the dish, and serve.

ESTIMATED PREPARATION TIME: 15 minutes.

1 cup nonfat plain yogurt
¼ cup fat-free cream cheese, softened
¼ cup honey
1 package (16 ounces) fresh carrot sticks
1 small bunch celery, trimmed and sliced into strips
2 cups fresh broccoli florets

131 Calories
4.6 g Protein
29.8 g Carbohydrates
0.3 g Fat
3.7 g Fiber
157 mg Sodium
1 mg Cholesterol

Easy Skewered Vegetables

Yield: 5 servings

1 cup fresh broccoli florets
1 cup fresh cauliflower
  florets
½ pound fresh Italian
  green beans, trimmed
  and cut into 1½-inch
  pieces
10 cherry tomatoes,
  stemmed and halved
2 tablespoons fat-free
  Italian dressing

Skewer vegetables on wooden skewers, alternating for a colorful presentation. Place in a 13- × 9-inch glass baking dish, drizzle Italian dressing over vegetables, cover with plastic wrap, and chill.

ESTIMATED PREPARATION TIME: 15 minutes.

Note: These skewered vegetables can be grilled, if desired. You can also use other fresh vegetables, such as zucchini, carrots, summer squash, etc. (Avoid carrot slices for younger children—they present a choking hazard.)

38 Calories
2.2 g Protein
7.7 g Carbohydrates
0.8 g Fat
2.4 g Fiber
97 mg Sodium
0 mg Cholesterol

Busy Mom's Lowfat Cookbook

Cauliflower Citrus Salad

Yield: 4 servings

Place cauliflower and orange slices in a medium bowl. In a small bowl, stir together lemonade concentrate, vinegar, and honey until honey is dissolved. Pour over cauliflower and oranges. Toss and chill. Serve on lettuce leaves.

ESTIMATED PREPARATION TIME: 5 minutes.

1 package (10 ounces) frozen cauliflower florets, thawed
1 can (11 ounces) mandarin orange slices, drained
¼ cup frozen lemonade concentrate, thawed
1 tablespoon white vinegar
1 tablespoon honey
4 lettuce leaves, rinsed and trimmed

86 Calories
1.7 g Protein
21.3 g Carbohydrates
0.2 g Fat
1.5 g Fiber
9 mg Sodium
0 mg Cholesterol

Quick Cabbage Patch Salad

Yield: 6 servings

½ small green cabbage
½ small red cabbage
2 large carrots
2 tablespoons white
    vinegar
2 tablespoons fat-free sour
    cream
2 tablespoons reduced-fat
    salad dressing or
    mayonnaise
¼ teaspoon salt
    pepper

Shred cabbage and carrots in food processor. Whisk together remaining ingredients and pour over vegetables. Toss and chill.

ESTIMATED PREPARATION TIME: 10 minutes.

51 Calories
2.1 g Protein
10.4 g Carbohydrates
1.0 g Fat
3.2 g Fiber
124 mg Sodium
0 mg Cholesterol

Busy Mom's Lowfat Cookbook

Easy Carrot Raisin Salad

Yield: 6 servings

Mix together carrots, raisins, and pineapple in a medium bowl and toss well. Combine the remaining ingredients in a small bowl, stirring well. Add to carrot mixture, mixing well. Cover and chill.

ESTIMATED PREPARATION TIME: 15 minutes.

2 cups coarsely shredded carrots
⅓ cup raisins
1 can (8 ounces) crushed pineapple in juice, drained
¼ cup nonfat aspartame-sweetened vanilla yogurt
2 tablespoons nonfat salad dressing or mayonnaise
1½ teaspoons reduced-fat creamy peanut butter

84 Calories
1.7 g Protein
19.5 g Carbohydrates
0.6 g Fat
2.1 g Fiber
92 mg Sodium
0 mg Cholesterol

Farmer John's Salad

Yield: 4 servings

1 package (10 ounces)
    frozen mixed
    vegetables
2 tablespoons fat-free
    French salad dressing
2 tablespoons nonfat plain
    yogurt
4 lettuce leaves, rinsed
    and trimmed
¼ cup reduced-fat
    Cheddar cheese,
    shredded

Microwave vegetables on High for 6 minutes. Stir in salad dressing and yogurt. Chill. To serve, spoon vegetables onto lettuce leaves and sprinkle with cheese.

ESTIMATED PREPARATION TIME: 5 minutes.

ESTIMATED COOKING TIME: 6 minutes.

127 Calories
6.9 g Protein
23.1 g Carbohydrates
1.5 g Fat
5.9 g Fiber
222 mg Sodium
5 mg Cholesterol

Fusilli Fruit and Vegetable Salad

Yield: 6 to 8 servings

Drain the pineapple, reserving 2 tablespoons of the liquid. Combine pasta, pineapple, cantaloupe, raisins, and vegetables in a medium bowl, cover, and chill for at least 30 minutes.

Whisk together yogurt and reserved pineapple juice. Chill.

Just before serving, slice, core, and chop the apples (unpeeled). Add to the pasta, fruits, and vegetables, and toss gently. Spoon into individual serving bowls that have been lined with spinach leaves. Drizzle yogurt mixture over the salads, and serve.

ESTIMATED PREPARATION TIME: 20 minutes plus chilling time (plus at least 30 minutes).

1 can (8 ounces) pineapple chunks, in juice
2 cups cooked fusilli pasta (twirls)
1 cup diced cantaloupe
½ cup raisins
1 package (10 ounces) frozen peas and carrots, thawed
1 cup lowfat aspartame-sweetened pineapple yogurt
2 medium red apples
12 (approximately) spinach leaves

149 Calories
4.5 g Protein
33.4 g Carbohydrates
0.7 g Fat
2.4 g Fiber
45 mg Sodium
1 mg Cholesterol

Simply Potato Salad

Yield: 6 servings

2 cans (16 ounces each)
   diced new potatoes,
   drained
2 tablespoons chopped
   green onions
1 jar (2 ounces) diced
   pimiento, drained
¼ cup nonfat salad
   dressing or
   mayonnaise
¼ cup plain nonfat yogurt
1 tablespoon prepared
   mustard
1½ teaspoons sugar
1½ teaspoons white vinegar
¼ teaspoon celery seeds
⅛ teaspoon pepper

Gently mix together potatoes, green onions, and pimiento in a large bowl. Combine remaining ingredients in a small bowl, mixing well. Add mixture to potatoes, tossing gently. Cover and chill.

ESTIMATED PREPARATION TIME: 10 minutes.

75 Calories
2.0 g Protein
16.5 g Carbohydrates
0.3 g Fat
0.5 g Fiber
511 mg Sodium
0 mg Cholesterol

Busy Mom's Lowfat Cookbook

Kid-Pleasing Waldorf Salad

Yield: 4 servings

Place all ingredients in a large bowl and toss.

ESTIMATED PREPARATION TIME: 15 minutes.

3 large apples, cored and
   diced
1 cup celery, diced
2 cups seedless white
   grapes, halved
⅓ cup chopped walnuts
4 cups torn lettuce leaves
⅓ cup fat-free salad
   dressing or
   mayonnaise
¼ cup fat-free plain yogurt

216 Calories
3.8 g Protein
39.8 g Carbohydrates
6.9 g Fat
4.2 g Fiber
298 mg Sodium
0 mg Cholesterol

Italian Broccoli

Yield: 4 servings

1 package (10 ounces) frozen chopped broccoli or frozen broccoli florets
2 teaspoons olive oil
¼ cup shredded part-skim-milk mozzarella

Place broccoli in a microwavable baking dish. Microwave on High for 5 minutes. Drizzle olive oil onto broccoli and stir or toss to coat. Sprinkle cheese on top and microwave on Medium High for 2 minutes.

ESTIMATED PREPARATION TIME: 2 minutes.

ESTIMATED COOKING TIME: 7 minutes.

76 Calories
6.0 g Protein
7.6 g Carbohydrates
3.6 g Fat
3.6 g Fiber
66 mg Sodium
4 mg Cholesterol

Busy Mom's Lowfat Cookbook

Florida Citrus Broccoli

Yield: 6 servings

Place broccoli in a microwavable serving bowl and microwave on Medium High for 8 minutes, stirring once after 4 minutes.

In a small nonstick saucepan, melt margarine over medium heat. Add flour and continue stirring until smooth. Cook for one minute more, stirring constantly. Combine orange rind and orange juice, then gradually add orange juice mixture to flour mixture, stirring constantly until mixture thickens and is bubbly. Pour sauce over broccoli.

- 2 packages (10 ounces each) frozen broccoli florets
- 1 tablespoon reduced-fat margarine
- 1 tablespoon all-purpose flour
- 1 teaspoon grated orange rind
- ¾ cup prepared orange juice

ESTIMATED PREPARATION TIME: 5 minutes.

ESTIMATED COOKING TIME: 15 minutes.

79 Calories
6.1 g Protein
14.4 g Carbohydrates
1.2 g Fat
4.9 g Fiber
68 mg Sodium
0 mg Cholesterol

Corny Confetti

Yield: 8 servings

2 packages (10 ounces each) frozen sweet corn, thawed and drained

¼ cup chopped green onions

1 jar (7 ounces) red pepper slices, drained

1 can (6 ounces) sliced ripe olives, drained

¼ cup mild salsa

Combine all ingredients in a microwavable casserole dish. Microwave on Medium High for 8 minutes, turning once at 4 minutes.

Note: Keeps well in the refrigerator for up to 10 days. Any leftovers can also be used as taco filling.

ESTIMATED PREPARATION TIME: 5 minutes.

ESTIMATED COOKING TIME: 8 minutes.

130 Calories
3.9 g Protein
27.1 g Carbohydrates
2.8 g Fat
3.4 g Fiber
294 mg Sodium
0 mg Cholesterol

Spicy Polynesian Carrots

Yield: 8 servings

In a medium nonstick pot, melt margarine over medium heat. Add pineapple juice, sugar, nutmeg, salt, carrots, and onion, then bring to a boil. Cover, reduce heat, and simmer 10 to 12 minutes, or until carrots begin to get tender. Using a slotted spoon, transfer vegetables to a serving dish and sprinkle with parsley.

ESTIMATED PREPARATION TIME: 2 minutes.

ESTIMATED COOKING TIME: 20 minutes.

2 tablespoons reduced-fat margarine
½ cup unsweetened pineapple juice
1 tablespoon brown sugar
½ teaspoon ground nutmeg
⅛ teaspoon salt
2 packages (10 ounces each) frozen carrots
1 medium onion, thinly sliced and separated into rings
1 teaspoon parsley flakes

76 Calories
1.6 g Protein
14.7 g Carbohydrates
1.6 g Fat
2.0 g Fiber
133 mg Sodium
0 mg Cholesterol

Southern-Style Green Beans

Yield: 4 to 6 servings

1 package (16 ounces)
   frozen green beans
1 cup water
1 teaspoon beef bouillon
   granules (or 1 cube)
1 medium onion, chopped
⅓ cup chopped turkey
   ham
¾ teaspoon salt
¼ teaspoon pepper

Place all ingredients in a saucepan and bring to a boil over medium heat. Cover, reduce heat, and simmer for 15 minutes or until beans are tender, stirring occasionally.

ESTIMATED PREPARATION TIME: 5 minutes.

ESTIMATED COOKING TIME: 20 minutes.

42 Calories
3.0 g Protein
7.1 g Carbohydrates
0.6 g Fat
2.5 g Fiber
499 mg Sodium
10 mg Cholesterol

Quick Snow Peas and Carrots

Yield: 4 servings

Place vegetables in a microwavable casserole dish. Microwave on High for 8 minutes, then toss gently. Add margarine and lemon juice. Microwave for an additional minute. Toss, top with almonds, and serve.

ESTIMATED PREPARATION TIME: 2 minutes.

ESTIMATED COOKING TIME: 9 minutes.

1 package (7 ounces) frozen Chinese snow peas
1 package (10 ounces) frozen carrots
1 tablespoon reduced-fat margarine
1 tablespoon lemon juice
¼ cup slivered almonds

101 Calories
3.9 g Protein
10.9 g Carbohydrates
5.3 g Fat
3.1 g Fiber
78 mg Sodium
0 mg Cholesterol

Minty Peas

Yield: 4 to 6 servings

1 package (16 ounces) frozen peas
2 teaspoons fresh mint, minced
2 tablespoons sugar
1 teaspoon reduced-fat margarine

Place all ingredients in a microwavable bowl or casserole dish. Cover and microwave on High for 6 to 8 minutes, stirring once after 3 minutes.

ESTIMATED PREPARATION TIME: 2 minutes.

ESTIMATED COOKING TIME: 8 minutes.

71 Calories
4.1 g Protein
12.7 g Carbohydrates
0.6 g Fat
1.7 g Fiber
78 mg Sodium
0 mg Cholesterol

Sweet and Creamy Potatoes

Yield: 6 to 8 servings

Wash sweet potatoes and slice off the ends of each. Cut in half and place cut side down on a microwavable plate that has been lightly coated with cooking spray. Microwave on High for a period of 4 minutes per potato (example: if your microwave holds only 2 potatoes, then microwave for a total of 8 minutes, repeating the process for the next two potatoes). Allow to cool slightly.

Using a spoon, scoop the potato pulp out of the skins. Place in a large mixing bowl. Add the softened margarine, milk, maple syrup, and ground cinnamon. Using an electric mixer or whisk, beat until creamy and smooth. Reheat in microwave oven if necessary.

4 large sweet potatoes
¼ cup reduced-fat margarine, softened
¼ cup skim milk
¼ cup maple syrup
¼ teaspoon ground cinnamon

ESTIMATED PREPARATION TIME: 15 minutes.

ESTIMATED COOKING TIME: 20 minutes.

140 Calories
1.7 g Protein
27.3 g Carbohydrates
3.0 g Fat
2.6 g Fiber
83 mg Sodium
0 mg Cholesterol

Sesame Spinach

Yield: 4 servings

1 pound fresh spinach
1 tablespoon toasted
    sesame seeds
1 teaspoon lemon juice
¼ teaspoon salt

Wash and trim spinach leaves, then pat dry with paper towels. Lightly coat a medium nonstick pot with cooking oil spray and place over medium heat. Add spinach. Cover and cook until spinach wilts, stirring occasionally. Remove from heat. Add sesame seeds, lemon juice, and salt. Toss gently and serve.

ESTIMATED PREPARATION TIME: 5 minutes.

ESTIMATED COOKING TIME: 10 minutes.

37 Calories
3.6 g Protein
4.6 g Carbohydrates
1.5 g Fat
3.0 g Fiber
221 mg Sodium
0 mg Cholesterol

Busy Mom's Lowfat Cookbook

Quick Stuffed Tomatoes

Yield: 6 servings

Remove stem ends of tomatoes and scoop out pulp with a spoon. In a medium bowl, mix pulp with croutons and cheese. Spoon mixture into tomatoes. Arrange tomatoes in a microwavable casserole dish and microwave on High for 5 minutes or until cheese has melted.

6 medium tomatoes
1 cup herbed croutons
½ cup reduced-fat shredded mozzarella cheese

ESTIMATED PREPARATION TIME: 10 minutes.

ESTIMATED COOKING TIME: 5 minutes.

67 Calories
5.0 g Protein
8.8 g Carbohydrates
2.1 g Fat
1.8 g Fiber
82 mg Sodium
2 mg Cholesterol

Golden Zucchini Sticks

Yield: 6 servings

4 or 5 medium-sized
   zucchini
1 egg white
⅔ cup flour
1 tablespoon cornstarch
½ teaspoon salt
¼ teaspoon pepper (if
   desired)

Preheat oven to 400 degrees. Lightly coat a baking sheet with cooking spray. Wash and dry zucchini. Trim off stems and cut in half lengthwise. Slice into ¼-inch strips to resemble French fries. Beat egg white until creamy. Stop beating just as soft peaks begin to form. Add zucchini strips and toss to coat evenly with egg white.

Place flour, cornstarch, salt, and pepper (if desired) in a large clean paper bag and shake vigorously. Drop small handfuls of the zucchini strips into the bag, close, and shake gently to coat. Place on prepared baking sheet, and repeat process until all strips are assembled on the sheet.

Bake for 12 to 15 minutes, or until golden brown. Serve with dipping sauces such as catsup, barbecue sauce, or honey.

ESTIMATED PREPARATION TIME: 10 minutes.

ESTIMATED COOKING TIME: 15 minutes.

HIGH ALTITUDE NOTE: Increase oven temperature to 425 degrees.

82 Calories
4.0 g Protein
17.0 g Carbohydrates
0.4 g Fat
2.5 g Fiber
192 mg Sodium
0 mg Cholesterol

Busy Mom's Lowfat Cookbook

Chapter 6

"Don't Worry, Be Happy" Dinners

West Texas Gumbo

Easy Beef Stew

Quick Taco Salad

Grilled Brisket Dinner

Oven-Fried Pork Chops

Sausage and Kraut Casserole

Quick Sausage Pizza

Crispy Oven-Fried Catfish

Pacific Grilled Salmon

Garlic and Lemon Shrimp

Easy Scallop Stir-Fry

General Cluck's "Fried" Chicken

Chicken Enchilada Pie

Easy Chinese Drumsticks

Easy Tortellini Alfredo

Best-Ever Veggie Burgers

Vegetable Tacos

Penne and Tomatoes

Fast Spaghetti Salad

Easy Vegetable Pizza

You've been stuck in rush-hour traffic for almost 45 minutes. The kids are hungry and cranky, and they're bickering in the back seat. Overflow work fills your attaché case, and you know it's going to be a long night. The last thing you want or need is to spend half the evening in the kitchen preparing dinner.

Fortunately, you won't have to. You can prepare a tasty meal in less time than it takes for pizza delivery, and cleanup is a snap. No, I'm not talking about canned ravioli or tuna fish sandwiches. The following recipes each use 10 or fewer ingredients, and they are low in fat, high in nutrition, and ready to serve in about 30 minutes.

Is it too hot to cook? A few of the recipes don't require an oven or stove. Whatever your mood or situation, there should be a recipe in this section that will take the worry out of dinner and help you enjoy a happy meal with your family.

West Texas Gumbo

Yield: 4 to 6 servings

Place ground chuck in a medium pot and brown over medium-high heat, stirring frequently. Carefully drain off excess fat.

Stir in peas, vegetables, water, bouillon, and rice, and bring to a boil. Reduce heat to low and simmer uncovered for 15 minutes, stirring occasionally. Serve with hot sauce, if desired.

ESTIMATED PREPARATION TIME: 10 minutes.

ESTIMATED COOKING TIME: 20 minutes.

1 pound ground chuck
1 can (15 ounces) black-eyed peas
1 package (16 ounces) frozen gumbo vegetable mix, thawed
2 cups water
2 teaspoons beef bouillon granules (or 2 cubes)
1 cup uncooked Minute rice
hot sauce

409 Calories
31.9 g Protein
32.7 g Carbohydrates
16.0 g Fat
3.7 g Fiber
707 mg Sodium
81 mg Cholesterol

"Don't Worry, Be Happy" Dinners

Easy Beef Stew

Yield: 6 servings

1 pound beef cube steaks
2 tablespoons canola oil
½ cup chopped onion
1 package (10 ounces) frozen mixed vegetables, partially thawed
4 small unpeeled new potatoes, diced
1 jar (16 ounces) reduced-fat beef gravy

Cut steaks into bite-sized pieces. Preheat a nonstick skillet over medium-high heat. Pour in oil, add meat and onions, and cook for 5 minutes, stirring frequently until browned. Stir in vegetables and potatoes. Pour gravy over meat and vegetables. Stir and cook until gravy begins to bubble. Reduce heat to low, cover, and simmer for 10 to 15 minutes or until potatoes are tender.

ESTIMATED PREPARATION TIME: 10 minutes.

ESTIMATED COOKING TIME: 20 minutes.

236 Calories
8.1 g Protein
36.8 g Carbohydrates
7.1 g Fat
7.7 g Fiber
470 mg Sodium
6 mg Cholesterol

Quick Taco Salad

Yield: 4 to 6 servings

Preheat large nonstick skillet over medium-high heat. Crumble ground beef into hot skillet and add onion. Cook until meat is browned and onion is translucent. Sprinkle chili powder, salt, and pepper over meat and onions, stirring to coat evenly. Remove from heat.

To serve, place a handful of tortilla chips in individual bowls. Add lettuce. Spoon spiced meat onto lettuce. Spoon tomatoes over meat and sprinkle with cheese. If desired, garnish with sliced black olives and lowfat sour cream.

1 pound lean ground beef
½ cup diced onion
½ teaspoon chili powder
½ teaspoon salt
¼ teaspoon pepper
  baked tortilla chips
4 cups torn lettuce
2 cups diced fresh
  tomatoes
1 cup reduced-fat
  shredded Cheddar
  cheese

ESTIMATED PREPARATION TIME: 15 minutes.

ESTIMATED COOKING TIME: 10 minutes.

709 Calories
28.3 g Protein
100.4 g Carbohydrates
20.4 g Fat
7.2 g Fiber
381 mg Sodium
66 mg Cholesterol

Grilled Brisket Dinner

Yield: 4 complete servings

1½ to 2 pounds beef brisket, trimmed
1 bottle zesty fat-free Italian dressing
2 large sweet potatoes
1 package (10 ounces) frozen green beans, thawed
1 can (21 ounces) pineapple slices in juice

In the morning: Place brisket in a 13- × 9-inch glass baking dish. Pour Italian dressing over meat, cover with plastic wrap, and refrigerate.

In the evening: Light charcoal in a grill. Wash the sweet potatoes and cut in half lengthwise. Drain green beans and wrap tightly in foil. Drain canned pineapple, reserving juice. When coals are hot, remove brisket from marinade and place in the center of grill. Discard marinade. Arrange sweet potatoes, cut side down, along the sides of the brisket. Place the foil pouch containing the green beans on the grill. Lower the grill cover and cook for 10 minutes.

Lift cover and brush meat and sweet potatoes with reserved pineapple juice. Lower cover and cook for an additional 5 minutes. Lift cover, turn meat, brush with reserved pineapple juice, and cook for another 5 minutes. Brush brisket again with the last of the pineapple juice. Turn sweet potatoes and place pineapple slices on grill, turning them once after 2 minutes.

Remove foil pouch from grill and transfer green beans to a serving dish. Remove pineapple and sweet potatoes to dinner plates. Place brisket on a serving platter, slice, and serve.

ESTIMATED PREPARATION TIME: 10 minutes plus marinade time.

ESTIMATED COOKING TIME: 25 minutes.

510 Calories
44.0 g Protein
53.8 g Carbohydrates
13.8 g Fat
6.7 g Fiber
267 mg Sodium
122 mg Cholesterol

Busy Mom's Lowfat Cookbook

Oven-Fried Pork Chops

Yield: 4 servings

Preheat oven to 400 degrees. Rinse pork chops under cold water and pat dry with paper towels. In a small bowl, combine mayonnaise and lemon juice; whisk until smooth. Place dry ingredients in a round cake pan or pie tin and stir. Lightly brush the pork chops with the lemon and mayonnaise mixture. Place in crumb mixture and coat evenly.

Arrange chops on cookie sheet that has been lightly coated with cooking oil spray. Bake on top rack of oven for 20 to 25 minutes.

4 pork loin chops, trimmed
2 tablespoons fat-free mayonnaise
1 tablespoon lemon juice
½ cup corn meal
¼ cup flour
¼ cup plain bread crumbs
½ teaspoon salt
¼ teaspoon pepper

ESTIMATED PREPARATION TIME: 10 minutes.

ESTIMATED COOKING TIME: 20 minutes.

319 Calories
30.3 g Protein
26.0 g Carbohydrates
9.5 g Fat
1.3 g Fiber
472 mg Sodium
84 mg Cholesterol

Sausage and Kraut Casserole

Yield: 6 servings

1 small head cabbage
¼ cup white wine vinegar
¼ cup dry white wine
2 tablespoons honey
2 tablespoons reduced-fat
    margarine
½ cup white onion, minced
    salt and pepper to taste
1 pound reduced-fat
    kielbasa sausage

Remove core and shred the cabbage into fine strips. Place in a glass or plastic (not metal) bowl. In a small bowl, stir together vinegar, wine, and honey until honey is dissolved. Pour over the cabbage and let sit for at least 30 minutes (or all day in the refrigerator if preparing in the morning).

Heat the margarine in a nonstick skillet over low heat. When the margarine has melted, add minced onion and sauté over low heat until the onion is translucent. Fold this into the cabbage mixture. Add salt and pepper to taste.

Preheat oven to 375 degrees. Place the cabbage mixture in a glass or Pyrex baking dish, lay the sausage on top, and bake (uncovered) for 15 minutes. Turn sausages and bake for an additional 10 minutes. Serve with rolls or biscuits.

160 Calories
14.9 g Protein
16.9 g Carbohydrates
3.4 g Fat
2.6 g Fiber
879 mg Sodium
20 mg Cholesterol

ESTIMATED PREPARATION TIME: 15 minutes plus marinade time.

ESTIMATED COOKING TIME: 25 minutes.

Busy Mom's Lowfat Cookbook

Quick Sausage Pizza

Yield: 6 servings

Preheat oven to 450 degrees. Place Italian bread shell on a nonstick cookie sheet. Combine tomatoes, catsup, and seasoning in a medium bowl, then spread on bread shell. Sprinkle cheese on top, then arrange sausage slices on the cheese. Bake for 10 minutes.

ESTIMATED PREPARATION TIME: 10 minutes.

ESTIMATED COOKING TIME: 10 minutes.

1 purchased Italian bread shell
1 can (15 ounces) diced tomatoes, drained
¼ cup catsup
1 teaspoon Italian herb mix
¾ cup reduced-fat shredded mozzarella cheese
½ pound "lite" turkey sausage, sliced thin

204 Calories
15.3 g Protein
23.1 g Carbohydrates
6.2 g Fat
1.1 g Fiber
763 mg Sodium
25 mg Cholesterol

Crispy Oven-Fried Catfish

Yield: 4 servings

1 package (8 ounces)
    corn muffin mix
¼ teaspoon chili powder
⅛ teaspoon pepper
¼ teaspoon salt
¼ cup fat-free French
    salad dressing
1 pound catfish fillets

Preheat oven to 450 degrees. Lightly coat a nonstick cookie sheet with a cooking oil spray.

In a medium bowl, combine corn muffin mix and seasonings, mixing well. Lightly brush fish with the dressing, coating evenly. Dip the fish into the cornmeal mixture and coat on all sides.

Place coated fillets on the cookie sheet and spray tops lightly with cooking oil spray. Bake for 15 minutes.

ESTIMATED PREPARATION TIME: 15 minutes.

ESTIMATED COOKING TIME: 15 minutes.

279 Calories
19.5 g Protein
32.1 g Carbohydrates
7.4 g Fat
2.5 g Fiber
999 mg Sodium
57 mg Cholesterol

Busy Mom's Lowfat Cookbook

Pacific Grilled Salmon

Yield: 6 servings

Light charcoal in a grill. Cut off heavy-duty aluminum foil at a length 6 inches longer than the fish. Lay the foil shiny side up, and coat lightly with cooking oil spray. Place fish in center of the foil and arrange onion and lemon slices on top. Squeeze the juice from the lemon halves over the fish. Arrange fresh parsley over onion and lemon.

Pull up the long edges of the foil and wrap tightly, folding down toward the center. Roll the ends of the foil tightly. Place fish on a hot grill, lower grill cover, and cook for 10 to 12 minutes.

1 whole salmon
   (3 pounds)
1 small red onion, sliced
   into thin rings
2 lemons, 1 halved,
   1 sliced
1 small bunch fresh
   parsley

ESTIMATED PREPARATION TIME: 15 minutes.

ESTIMATED COOKING TIME: 10 minutes.

326 Calories
44.3 g Protein
1.9 g Carbohydrates
14.3 g Fat
0.6 g Fiber
103 mg Sodium
122 mg Cholesterol

Garlic and Lemon Shrimp

Yield: 4 servings

1 pound medium-sized
shrimp, peeled and
deveined
1 teaspoon minced garlic
¼ cup lemon juice
4 cups cooked rice

Preheat a large nonstick skillet over medium heat. Lightly coat with cooking oil spray. Place shrimp into the hot skillet and stir-fry for 5 minutes or until shrimp is pink. Add garlic and stir-fry for an additional minute. Pour lemon juice into skillet, and stir to deglaze (lightly loosening any food from the bottom of the pan). Reduce heat and simmer for 1 to 2 minutes, stirring constantly. Remove from heat and serve over rice.

ESTIMATED PREPARATION TIME: 5 minutes.

ESTIMATED COOKING TIME: 8 minutes.

365 Calories
25.1 g Protein
59.5 g Carbohydrates
1.8 g Fat
1.2 g Fiber
212 mg Sodium
181 mg Cholesterol

Easy Scallop Stir-Fry

Yield: 4 servings

Pour cornstarch, white wine, soy sauce, water, and bouillon into a small glass bowl and whisk to combine.

Preheat a large nonstick skillet over medium-high heat, then lightly coat skillet with cooking oil spray. Place scallops in hot skillet and stir-fry 5 to 7 minutes or until scallops are opaque. Remove from skillet.

Place vegetables in skillet and stir-fry for 5 to 7 minutes. Return scallops to skillet and pour cornstarch mixture over scallops and vegetables. Cook, stirring constantly, until sauce thickens. Serve over rice.

ESTIMATED PREPARATION TIME: 5 minutes.

ESTIMATED COOKING TIME: 15 minutes.

2 tablespoons cornstarch
3 tablespoons dry white wine
¼ cup soy sauce
1 cup water
1 teaspoon chicken bouillon granules (or 1 cube)
2 cups fresh sea scallops
1 package (16 ounces) frozen stir-fry vegetables, thawed and drained
4 cups cooked rice

478 Calories
26.6 g Protein
75.0 g Carbohydrates
7.0 g Fat
2.7 g Fiber
1860 mg Sodium
34 mg Cholesterol

General Cluck's "Fried" Chicken

Yield: 6 to 8 crispy servings

2 pounds boneless,
  skinless chicken
  (breasts or thighs)
½ cup fat-free
  mayonnaise
½ cup fat-free Ranch salad
  dressing
1 cup unseasoned bread
  crumbs
½ cup finely crushed corn
  flakes
¼ teaspoon pepper

Preheat oven to 400 degrees. Lightly coat baking sheet with cooking spray. Place chicken pieces in a large bowl filled with cold water.

In a casserole dish or wide bowl, whip together the mayonnaise and dressing. In another dish, stir together bread crumbs, corn flakes, and pepper until evenly combined.

Using a serving fork, remove chicken pieces, one at a time, and dip them in the mayonnaise mixture. Coat each piece evenly. Remove carefully with the fork and roll each piece in the crumb coating mix. Shake gently to remove excess, and place on baking sheet.

Bake for 20 minutes, or until golden brown.

ESTIMATED PREPARATION TIME: 10 minutes.

ESTIMATED COOKING TIME: 20 minutes.

HIGH ALTITUDE NOTE: Add 1 tablespoon flour to the bread crumb mixture. Increase cooking time by 5 minutes.

284 Calories
35.1 g Protein
22.3 g Carbohydrates
4.6 g Fat
0.5 g Fiber
599 mg Sodium
90 mg Cholesterol

Busy Mom's Lowfat Cookbook

Chicken Enchilada Pie

Yield: 6 servings

In a large bowl, combine chicken, tomatoes, Cheddar cheese, and ¾ cup of the Monterey Jack cheese. Lightly coat an 8-inch diameter microwavable casserole dish with cooking oil spray. Place one tortilla in bottom of dish. Spoon ¼ of the chicken mixture onto the tortilla and spread evenly. Place another tortilla in the casserole, covering the chicken mixture. Continue layering until all tortillas and filling have been used.

Sprinkle the remaining Monterey jack cheese on top, cover, and microwave on High for 7 to 9 minutes. Slice and serve with a dollop of sour cream and an olive as garnish on each slice.

3 cups diced cooked
   chicken breast
2 cans (15 ounces) diced
   tomatoes with chilies
1 cup fat-free shredded
   Cheddar cheese
1 cup reduced-fat
   shredded Monterey
   Jack cheese
5 flour tortillas
½ cup fat-free sour cream
   ripe olives for garnish

ESTIMATED PREPARATION TIME: 15 minutes.

ESTIMATED COOKING TIME: 9 minutes.

303 Calories
35.6 g Protein
22.2 g Carbohydrates
7.9 g Fat
1.9 g Fiber
515 mg Sodium
70 mg Cholesterol

Easy Chinese Drumsticks

Yield: 4 servings

8 chicken drumsticks
⅓ cup orange marmalade
1 tablespoon Chinese hot
   mustard
2 tablespoons soy sauce

Preheat oven to 400 degrees. Lightly coat a 9-inch square pan with cooking oil spray and arrange drumsticks in pan. Combine remaining ingredients in a small bowl and stir well. Spoon the mixture over the drumsticks and spread to coat well. Bake uncovered for 15 minutes. Cover with foil and continue baking for an additional 10 minutes.

ESTIMATED PREPARATION TIME: 5 minutes.

ESTIMATED COOKING TIME: 25 minutes.

306 Calories
28.8 g Protein
17.0 g Carbohydrates
12.0 g Fat
0 g Fiber
656 mg Sodium
96 mg Cholesterol

Busy Mom's Lowfat Cookbook

Easy Tortellini Alfredo

Yield: 4 servings

Prepare tortellini according to package directions. Place frozen peas in microwavable bowl or baking dish, cover, and microwave on High for 7 minutes; drain.

Pour Alfredo sauce into a medium-sized nonstick pot. Add cooked tortellini, peas, and chopped onion. Cook until sauce begins to bubble, stirring occasionally. Remove from heat, transfer into serving bowl, and sprinkle with fresh basil.

ESTIMATED PREPARATION TIME: 10 minutes.

ESTIMATED COOKING TIME: 20 minutes.

1 package (9 ounces) fresh cheese-and-basil tortellini
1 package (10 ounces) frozen peas
1 tub (10 ounces) prepared "light" Alfredo sauce
½ cup chopped green onion
1 tablespoon chopped fresh basil

333 Calories
16.3 g Protein
40.1 g Carbohydrates
12.6 g Fat
2.9 g Fiber
490 mg Sodium
96 mg Cholesterol

Best-Ever Veggie Burgers

Yield: 4 servings

4 frozen vegetarian "beef"
  patties
2 tablespoons soy sauce
2 tablespoons spicy steak
  sauce
1 tablespoon canola oil
4 whole wheat burger
  buns
4 teaspoons Special Sauce
  (recipe below)
4 lettuce leaves
4 thin slices tomato

Special Sauce
1 tablespoon fat-free
  mayonnaise
1 teaspoon catsup
1 teaspoon sweet relish

Brush both sides of each patty with soy sauce and steak sauce. Preheat medium skillet over medium-high heat. Add canola oil. Arrange patties in skillet and cook for 3 minutes. Turn and cook for an additional 2 minutes. Turn off burner and remove pan from heat.

Open burger buns and spread each with 1 teaspoon Special Sauce. Place patties on buns, top with lettuce and tomato, and serve.

For Special Sauce: Combine all ingredients.

ESTIMATED PREPARATION TIME: 10 minutes.

ESTIMATED COOKING TIME: 5 minutes.

386 Calories
22.0 g Protein
50.7 g Carbohydrates
10.6 g Fat
4.5 g Fiber
1414 mg Sodium
0 mg Cholesterol

Vegetable Tacos

Yield: 6 servings

Combine vegetables in microwavable casserole dish or bowl. Microwave on High for 3 minutes. Stir. Line bottom of each taco shell with lettuce. Spoon vegetables into taco shells and sprinkle with cheese. Top with a dollop each of sour cream and salsa.

ESTIMATED PREPARATION TIME: 15 minutes.

ESTIMATED COOKING TIME: 3 minutes.

1 can (16 ounces) whole-kernel corn, drained
1 cup diced zucchini
1 cup chopped tomato
6 taco shells
½ small head of lettuce, chopped
1 cup reduced-fat shredded Cheddar cheese
½ cup nonfat sour cream
½ cup mild salsa

164 Calories
9.7 g Protein
20.8 g Carbohydrates
6.1 g Fat
2.3 g Fiber
437 mg Sodium
13 mg Cholesterol

Penne and Tomatoes

Yield: 4 servings

1 teaspoon olive oil
1 teaspoon minced garlic
1 can (15 ounces) diced Italian-style tomatoes
2 cups uncooked penne pasta
¼ cup finely shredded Parmesan cheese

Preheat nonstick skillet over medium heat. Pour olive oil into hot skillet; add garlic and sauté for one minute. Add entire contents of canned tomatoes to skillet, and stir in one canful of water. Bring to a boil. Add pasta and reduce heat to low. Cover and simmer for 7 minutes.

Remove cover, stir, and simmer until most of the liquid has been absorbed. Transfer to serving bowl and sprinkle with cheese.

ESTIMATED PREPARATION TIME: 5 minutes.

ESTIMATED COOKING TIME: 15 minutes.

250 Calories
9.9 g Protein
44.5 g Carbohydrates
3.7 g Fat
1.9 g Fiber
281 mg Sodium
4 mg Cholesterol

Busy Mom's Lowfat Cookbook

Fast Spaghetti Salad

Yield: 5 servings

Place spaghetti, onion, pepper, and tomato in a large mixing or salad bowl. In a small bowl, combine mayonnaise and Italian dressing. Pour over pasta and vegetables and toss well. Cover and chill for several hours. Sprinkle with seasoned croutons before serving.

ESTIMATED PREPARATION TIME: 15 minutes + chilling time.

5 cups cooked spaghetti
2 medium red onions, diced fine
2 medium green bell peppers, cored, seeded, and sliced thin
2 small tomatoes, diced
½ cup fat-free mayonnaise
1 cup nonfat zesty Italian dressing
1 cup seasoned croutons

296 Calories
8.7 g Protein
55.5 g Carbohydrates
5.7 g Fat
4.2 g Fiber
1048 mg Sodium
0 mg Cholesterol

Easy Vegetable Pizza

Yield: 4 to 6 servings

1 purchased Italian bread shell
1 can (15 ounces) chopped Italian-style tomatoes, drained
2 tablespoons catsup
1 cup reduced-fat mozzarella cheese
¼ cup chopped onion
1 cup shredded carrot
1 cup shredded zucchini
1 cup sliced mushrooms
1 small red bell pepper, cored, seeded, and sliced into thin rings

Preheat oven to 450 degrees. Place bread shell on cookie sheet. Combine tomatoes and catsup and spread onto bread shell. Sprinkle cheese over tomatoes. Assemble vegetables on top of cheese. Bake 10 minutes.

ESTIMATED PREPARATION TIME: 15 minutes.

ESTIMATED COOKING TIME: 10 minutes.

174 Calories
12.4 g Protein
24.8 g Carbohydrates
3.9 g Fat
2.3 g Fiber
386 mg Sodium
6 mg Cholesterol

Busy Mom's Lowfat Cookbook

Chapter 7

What a Crock!

Family Pot Roast	Sweet and Sour Chicken
Irish Beef and Cabbage	Holiday Turkey Roast
German-Style Short Ribs	Easy Turkey Chili
Tender Teriyaki	Boston Baked Beans
New England Boiled Dinner	Simply Cassoulet
Easy Beef Stroganoff	Lentil Soup
Malaysian Pork	Great Pumpkin Soup
Holiday Pork Roast	Alphabet Beef Soup
Sweet and Spicy Ham	Tortilla Soup
Country Kielbasa and Cabbage	Corn Chowder

Imagine this: you've been running at warp speed all day, taking care of business, errands, carpools, and kids. But today, as the sun is slowly creeping toward the western horizon, you come home to find the aroma of a delicious meal. The table is set. Dinner is ready. Your loved ones gather 'round . . . and no one is bickering.

Okay. Siblings will be siblings. But for a one-time investment of about $20, and in the time it takes your coffee maker to do its thing in the morning, you can arrive home to a piping hot dinner—even if you're an hour or two late.

Crock-Pots are popular because they save time, money, and energy; they are easy to use and a snap to clean up. They're also ideal for today's lowfat menus. Each of the following recipes has simmered on my countertop and delighted my family. I hope you're also delighted with these fast meals in a slow cooker.

Family Pot Roast

Yield: 6 servings

Trim visible fat from meat. Rub all sides of meat with salt and lemon pepper. Place vegetables on bottom of a slow cooker. Pour soup over vegetables. Place seasoned meat on top of vegetables. Cover and cook on low for 8 to 9 hours or until meat and vegetables are tender.

ESTIMATED PREPARATION TIME: 10 minutes.

ESTIMATED COOKING TIME: 8 to 9 hours.

3 pounds beef rump roast
½ teaspoon salt
¼ teaspoon lemon pepper
1 onion, cut into 8 wedges
1 package (10 ounces) baby carrots
6 new potatoes, halved
1 celery stalk, diced
1 can (10¾ ounces) French Onion Soup

486 Calories
54.3 g Protein
30.4 g Carbohydrates
15.2 g Fat
3.1 g Fiber
825 mg Sodium
136 mg Cholesterol

Irish Beef and Cabbage

Yield: 6 to 8 servings

2 to 2½ pounds corned
    beef brisket
1 medium onion, chopped
1 package (10 ounces)
    frozen baby carrots
½ small cabbage,
    shredded
1 cup water
¼ cup red wine vinegar

Place corned beef in a slow cooker. Top with onion, carrots, water, and wine vinegar. Cover and cook on low for 8 to 9 hours or until meat is tender. Remove from cooker; slice and serve.

ESTIMATED PREPARATION TIME: **10 minutes.**

ESTIMATED COOKING TIME: **8 to 9 hours.**

266 Calories
18.2 g Protein
10.4 g Carbohydrates
17.1 g Fat
2.5 g Fiber
1420 mg Sodium
61 mg Cholesterol

Busy Mom's Lowfat Cookbook

German-Style Short Ribs

Yield: 5 or 6 servings

Place ribs in a slow cooker. Combine red wine vinegar, barbecue sauce, and mustard in a small bowl, and then pour over ribs. Cover and cook on low for 6 to 8 hours. Serve hot over noodles.

ESTIMATED PREPARATION TIME: 5 minutes.

ESTIMATED COOKING TIME: 6 to 8 hours.

3 to 3½ pounds beef short ribs, fat trimmed
¼ cup red wine vinegar
1 cup barbecue sauce
1 teaspoon prepared mustard
3 cups cooked wide noodles

797 Calories
27.2 g Protein
32.1 g Carbohydrates
24.4 g Fat
1.4 g Fiber
745 mg Sodium
129 mg Cholesterol

Tender Teriyaki

Yield: 6 to 8 servings

2 to 2½ pounds boneless chuck steak cut into strips
1 sweet red bell pepper, seeded and diced
¼ cup soy sauce
¼ teaspoon ground ginger
1 tablespoon honey
2 tablespoons canola oil
1 teaspoon chopped garlic
1 can (20 ounces) pineapple chunks in juice, drained
3 tablespoons cornstarch
3 tablespoons water
3 to 4 cups cooked rice

Place beef and bell pepper in a slow cooker. In a small bowl, combine soy sauce, ginger, honey, oil, and garlic. Pour sauce mixture over meat. Cover and cook on low for 6 to 7 hours.

Turn control to high. Stir in pineapple. Combine cornstarch and water in a small bowl and add to cooker. Cook, stirring, until slightly thickened. Serve over rice.

ESTIMATED PREPARATION TIME: 20 minutes.

ESTIMATED COOKING TIME: 6 to 7 hours.

384 Calories
27.7 g Protein
46.0 g Carbohydrates
9.5 g Fat
0.9 g Fiber
594 mg Sodium
68 mg Cholesterol

Busy Mom's Lowfat Cookbook

New England Boiled Dinner

Yield: 6 servings

Sprinkle the meat with the salt and pepper. Place frozen vegetables and potatoes in a slow cooker. Top with meat. Add vinegar and water. Cover and cook on low for 5 to 7 hours or until meat is tender. Remove meat.

Preheat oil in a nonstick saucepan. Stir in flour. Remove 1½ cups of beef broth from the slow cooker. Pour broth and horseradish into saucepan. Cook over low heat, stirring constantly, until thickened and smooth. Serve roast and vegetables with the sauce.

ESTIMATED PREPARATION TIME: 15 minutes.

ESTIMATED COOKING TIME: 5 to 7 hours.

3 pounds beef chuck roast
½ teaspoon salt
¼ teaspoon pepper
1 package New England-style frozen vegetables (pearl onions, celery, carrots, brussels sprouts)
6 to 8 small new potatoes
2 tablespoons vinegar
2 cups water
2 tablespoons canola oil
2 tablespoons all-purpose flour
2 tablespoons prepared horseradish

470 Calories
52.5 g Protein
28.6 g Carbohydrates
16.0 g Fat
4.3 g Fiber
371 mg Sodium
136 mg Cholesterol

Easy Beef Stroganoff

Yield: 6 or 7 servings

1½ to 2 pounds round steak
½ teaspoon salt
⅛ teaspoon pepper
1 onion, sliced
1 can (10½ ounces) cream of mushroom soup
1 tablespoon catsup
2 tablespoons red wine vinegar
1 cup fat-free sour cream
3 cups cooked rice or noodles

Cut steak into ¼-inch strips. Season with salt and pepper. Place steak and onion in a slow cooker. Combine condensed soup, catsup, and vinegar in a bowl. Pour mixture over steak. Cover and cook on low for 6 to 7 hours or until steak is tender. Stir in sour cream. Serve with rice or noodles.

ESTIMATED PREPARATION TIME: 10 minutes.

ESTIMATED COOKING TIME: 6 to 7 hours.

333 Calories
28.0 g Protein
36.6 g Carbohydrates
7.4 g Fat
1.0 g Fiber
598 mg Sodium
55 mg Cholesterol

Busy Mom's Lowfat Cookbook

Malaysian Pork

Yield: 6 servings

Place roast in a slow cooker. Sprinkle with salt and pepper. In a small bowl, combine honey, soy sauce, pepper flakes, and lemon juice. Pour mixture over meat. Sprinkle ginger over meat. Cover and cook on low for 9 to 10 hours. Remove meat and keep warm. Skim off excess fat from juices. Stir in peanut butter and cook for about 5 minutes on high. Serve with sauce over cooked rice.

4 to 5 pounds pork roast,
    fat trimmed
salt and pepper
¼ cup honey
¼ cup soy sauce
½ teaspoon dried red
    pepper flakes
¼ cup fresh lemon juice
1 teaspoon ground ginger
¾ cup reduced-fat crunchy
    peanut butter
cooked rice

ESTIMATED PREPARATION TIME: 5 minutes.

ESTIMATED COOKING TIME: 9 to 10 hours.

857	Calories
79.5 g	Protein
55.1 g	Carbohydrates
34.0 g	Fat
2.0 g	Fiber
1092 mg	Sodium
192 mg	Cholesterol

Holiday Pork Roast

Yield: 6 to 8 servings

3 to 4 pounds boneless or
    loin pork roast
salt and pepper
1 can (16 ounces)
    cranberry sauce
¼ cup unsweetened
    orange juice
⅛ teaspoon ground cloves
⅛ teaspoon nutmeg

Sprinkle roast with salt and pepper and place in a slow cooker. In a small bowl, combine remaining ingredients; pour over roast. Cover and cook on low for 8 to 10 hours or until roast is tender. Slice and serve hot.

Note: Great with sweet potatoes and salad!

ESTIMATED PREPARATION TIME: 5 minutes.

ESTIMATED COOKING TIME: 8 to 10 hours.

382 Calories
38.2 g Protein
27.8 g Carbohydrates
12.5 g Fat
0.2 g Fiber
133 mg Sodium
109 mg Cholesterol

Busy Mom's Lowfat Cookbook

Sweet and Spicy Ham

Yield: 8 to 10 servings

Stud ham with the whole cloves. Place ham in a slow cooker. Arrange yam cubes around the meat. Add pineapple, then sprinkle raisins into slow cooker. In a small bowl, combine water, vinegar, mustard, and cinnamon; pour over meat and yams. Cover and cook on low for 6 to 8 hours.

ESTIMATED PREPARATION TIME: 15 minutes.

ESTIMATED COOKING TIME: 6 to 8 hours.

5 to 7 pounds turkey ham
1 tablespoon whole cloves
2 large fresh yams, peeled and cubed
1 can (8 ounces) pineapple chunks, in juice
½ cup raisins
¼ cup water
1 tablespoon vinegar
½ teaspoon dry mustard
¼ teaspoon ground cinnamon

361 Calories
43.7 g Protein
18.2 g Carbohydrates
11.6 g Fat
1.4 g Fiber
2264 mg Sodium
288 mg Cholesterol

Country Kielbasa and Cabbage

Yield: 6 servings

1 pound reduced-fat
 kielbasa (Polish
 sausage)
1 onion, diced
1 small head cabbage,
 shredded
2 apples, cored and sliced
½ teaspoon salt
1 teaspoon celery seeds
2 teaspoons chicken
 bouillon granules
 (or 2 cubes)
1 cup hot water

Cut kielbasa into 2-inch chunks. In a slow cooker, arrange alternating layers of sausage with onion, cabbage, and apples. Sprinkle with salt and celery seeds. Dissolve bouillon in hot water and pour into slow cooker. Cover and cook on low for 5 to 6 hours or until cabbage is tender. Serve with a slotted spoon to drain off liquid.

ESTIMATED PREPARATION TIME: 15 minutes.

ESTIMATED COOKING TIME: 5 to 6 hours.

147 Calories
15.4 g Protein
18.7 g Carbohydrates
1.9 g Fat
3.8 g Fiber
1391 mg Sodium
20 mg Cholesterol

Sweet and Sour Chicken

Yield: 6 servings

Place chicken and onion in a slow cooker. In a small bowl, combine broth, brown sugar, vinegar, catsup, and salt. Pour mixture over chicken. Add bell pepper and pineapple chunks. Cover and cook on low for about 6 hours or until chicken is tender. Serve over rice.

ESTIMATED PREPARATION TIME: 10 minutes.

ESTIMATED COOKING TIME: about 6 hours.

2½ to 3 pounds skinless chicken thighs
1 small onion, thinly sliced
1 cup chicken broth
¼ cup packed brown sugar
¼ cup vinegar
1 tablespoon catsup
½ teaspoon salt
1 red bell pepper, cut into chunks
1 can (20 ounces) pineapple chunks in juice, drained

441 Calories
27.2 g Protein
30.4 g Carbohydrates
6.3 g Fat
0.8 g Fiber
488 mg Sodium
126 mg Cholesterol

Holiday Turkey Roast

Yield: 6 servings

¾ cup marmalade
1 can (16 ounces)
   cranberry sauce
1 turkey breast (2 to 2½
   pounds)
salt and pepper

In a small bowl, mix marmalade and cranberry sauce. Place turkey in a slow cooker and sprinkle lightly with salt and pepper. Pour sauce over turkey. Cover and cook on low for 6 to 8 hours. Slice turkey and spoon sauce over slices.

ESTIMATED PREPARATION TIME: 5 minutes.

ESTIMATED COOKING TIME: 6 to 8 hours.

420 Calories
35.8 g Protein
59.6 g Carbohydrates
2.5 g Fat
0.3 g Fiber
122 mg Sodium
91 mg Cholesterol

Busy Mom's Lowfat Cookbook

Easy Turkey Chili

Yield: 6 servings

Thoroughly combine all ingredients in a slow cooker. Cover and cook on low for 6 to 8 hours or until onion is tender.

ESTIMATED PREPARATION TIME: 5 minutes.

ESTIMATED COOKING TIME: 6 to 8 hours.

1 pound uncooked ground turkey
½ cup chopped onion
½ teaspoon salt
2 teaspoons chili powder
1 tablespoon steak sauce
1 can (15 ounces) crushed tomatoes
2 cans (16 ounces each) kidney beans, drained

253 Calories
22.0 g Protein
27.4 g Carbohydrates
6.5 g Fat
5.8 g Fiber
775 mg Sodium
56 mg Cholesterol

Boston Baked Beans

Yield: 6 to 8 servings

2 cups dried small white
  beans, rinsed
3½ cups water
⅓ cup dark molasses
¼ cup brown sugar
½ cup chopped onion
1 tablespoon canola oil
1 tablespoon prepared
  mustard

Combine all ingredients in a slow cooker. Cover and cook on low for 6 to 8 hours or until beans are tender.

ESTIMATED PREPARATION TIME: 5 minutes.

ESTIMATED COOKING TIME: 6 to 8 hours.

247 Calories
12.0 g Protein
45.5 g Carbohydrates
2.4 g Fat
2.9 g Fiber
53 mg Sodium
0 mg Cholesterol

Busy Mom's Lowfat Cookbook

Simply Cassoulet

Yield: 5 or 6 servings

In a slow cooker, combine chicken, onion, garlic, parsley, salt, and pepper. Top with beans and sausage. Add wine. Cover and cook on low for 5 to 6 hours or until chicken is tender.

ESTIMATED PREPARATION TIME: 10 minutes.

ESTIMATED COOKING TIME: 5 to 6 hours.

2½ to 3½ pounds chicken
   thighs and/or
   drumsticks
½ cup diced green onion
1 teaspoon minced garlic
3 tablespoons chopped
   fresh parsley or
   1 tablespoon parsley
   flakes
½ teaspoon salt
½ teaspoon pepper
2 cans (16 ounces each)
   kidney beans, drained
½ pound reduced-fat
   smoked sausage links,
   cut into ½-inch-thick
   slices
⅓ cup dry white wine

526 Calories
38.8 g Protein
23.5 g Carbohydrates
26.1 g Fat
5.1 g Fiber
962 mg Sodium
146 mg Cholesterol

Lentil Soup

Yield: 6 servings

1 cup lentils
1 tablespoon garlic-
  flavored oil
1 can (15 ounces) tomato
  sauce
1 teaspoon curry powder
½ cup chopped onion
4 cups water

Rinse lentils; pick out any debris. Place all ingredients in a slow cooker. Cover and cook on low for 7 to 8 hours or until lentils are tender.

ESTIMATED PREPARATION TIME: 5 minutes.

ESTIMATED COOKING TIME: 7 to 8 hours.

160 Calories
10.4 g Protein
25.5 g Carbohydrates
2.8 g Fat
5.1 g Fiber
473 mg Sodium
0 mg Cholesterol

Busy Mom's Lowfat Cookbook

Great Pumpkin Soup

Yield: 5 or 6 servings

Combine all ingredients in a slow cooker. Cover and cook on low for 9 to 9½ hours. Garnish with watercress leaves or parsley.

ESTIMATED PREPARATION TIME: 5 minutes.

ESTIMATED COOKING TIME: 9 to 9½ hours.

1 can (16 ounces) pumpkin
4 cups water
4 teaspoons chicken bouillon granules (or 4 cubes)
½ cup chopped green onion
3 tablespoons honey
½ teaspoon curry powder
½ teaspoon cayenne pepper
½ teaspoon salt
¼ cup frozen apple juice concentrate, thawed

89	Calories
1.6 g	Protein
21.2 g	Carbohydrates
0.4 g	Fat
1.5 g	Fiber
962 mg	Sodium
1 mg	Cholesterol

Alphabet Beef Soup

Yield: 6 or 7 servings

½ pound sirloin steak
1 can (16 ounces) Italian-style diced tomatoes
1 can (8 ounces) tomato sauce
3 cups water
3 beef bouillon cubes
1 package (16 ounces) frozen mixed vegetables
½ cup uncooked alphabet noodles

Cut meat into small cubes. In a slow cooker, combine meat, tomatoes, tomato sauce, water, bouillon, and vegetables. Cover and cook on low for 6 to 8 hours or until meat is tender. Turn control to high. Add noodles. Cover and cook on high for 15 to 20 minutes or until noodles are cooked.

ESTIMATED PREPARATION TIME: 10 minutes.

ESTIMATED COOKING TIME: 6 to 8 hours.

197 Calories
11.2 g Protein
24.4 g Carbohydrates
6.6 g Fat
3.3 g Fiber
739 mg Sodium
22 mg Cholesterol

Tortilla Soup

Yield: 6 servings

Combine chicken, onion, tomatoes, water, bouillon, and hot sauce in a slow cooker. Cover and cook on low for 7 to 8 hours. Heat oil in a large skillet. Add tortilla strips. Cook, stirring, over medium heat until crisp; drain on paper towels. Reheat soup if needed and spoon into individual bowls. Top with tortilla strips and sprinkle with cilantro.

ESTIMATED PREPARATION TIME: 20 minutes.

ESTIMATED COOKING TIME: 7 to 8 hours.

2 chicken breast halves, boned, skinned, and diced
½ cup chopped onion
1 can (15 ounces) diced tomatoes
4 cups water
4 teaspoons chicken bouillon (or 4 cubes)
2 tablespoons medium hot sauce or salsa
2 tablespoons canola oil
4 corn tortillas, halved and cut into ¼-inch strips
2 tablespoons coarsely chopped fresh cilantro

157 Calories
11.4 g Protein
14.7 g Carbohydrates
5.9 g Fat
1.6 g Fiber
985 mg Sodium
23 mg Cholesterol

Corn Chowder

Yield: 6 to 8 servings

2 packages (16 ounces each) frozen whole-kernel corn

2 medium potatoes, peeled and diced

½ cup chopped onion

½ teaspoon salt

⅛ teaspoon pepper

2 cups water

2 teaspoons chicken bouillon (or 2 cubes)

1 can (12 ounces) evaporated skim milk

¼ cup reduced-fat margarine

Combine corn, potatoes, onion, salt, pepper, water, and bouillon in a slow cooker. Cover and cook on low for 7 to 9 hours. Stir in milk and margarine. Cover and cook on high until soup begins to bubble.

ESTIMATED PREPARATION TIME: 20 minutes.

ESTIMATED COOKING TIME: 7 to 9 hours.

157 Calories
6.8 g Protein
27.7 g Carbohydrates
3.4 g Fat
2.3 g Fiber
553 mg Sodium
2 mg Cholesterol

Busy Mom's Lowfat Cookbook

Chapter 8

Bring On Dessert!

There's no need to tempt a child into eating dessert. Kids (and adults) love sweets. If it's a gooey treat, all the better! Yet we know that most desserts are laden with fat and sugar—things that aren't good for us.

Supermarkets everywhere now carry low-fat or no-fat versions of brownies, cookies, and cake mixes, but often taste is sacrificed for healthier eating. And the cost of those specialty products is unbelievable. A package of fat-free brownies can run almost $4! Fat-free sugarless frozen yogurt can cost almost $5 per carton—and have you read the label? You'd need to be a chemist to figure out what's in it.

I'll bet you didn't know that you can sneak the nutrition of vegetables and high-iron fruits into sinful-tasting goodies. Your children won't suspect (or care) that what they're gobbling contains essential vitamins, is low in both fat and sugar, and was a snap to prepare.

Best Fudgy Brownies

Yield: up to 12 servings

Preheat oven to 375 degrees. Place all ingredients in a large mixing bowl and stir vigorously until well combined. Lightly coat a 9-inch square baking dish with cooking oil spray. Pour batter into baking dish and spread evenly. Bake for 15 to 20 minutes. Let cool before serving.

ESTIMATED PREPARATION TIME: 5 minutes.

ESTIMATED COOKING TIME: 15 minutes.

HIGH ALTITUDE NOTE: Add 1 tablespoon flour and increase oven temperature to 400 degrees.

BROWNIE VARIATIONS

Prepare Best Fudgy Brownie recipe and stir in:
   Cherry: ¼ cup chopped maraschino cherries, drained.
   Coconut: ½ cup flaked coconut.
   Date: ½ cup chopped dates.
   Mocha: 2 teaspoons powdered instant coffee.
   Nut: ½ cup any dry roasted nuts.
Bake as above.

1 cup flour
½ cup sugar
1 teaspoon baking powder
1 teaspoon baking soda
2 tablespoons powdered cocoa
1 whole egg
1 egg white
1 jar (4 ounces) puréed prunes (baby food)
¼ cup water

85	Calories
2.0 g	Protein
17.7 g	Carbohydrates
0.9 g	Fat
0.3 g	Fiber
126 mg	Sodium
17 mg	Cholesterol

Easy Sour Cream Brownies

Yield: up to 20 servings

1 package (22½ ounces)
fudge brownie mix
¼ cup egg substitute
¾ cup nonfat sour cream

Preheat oven to 375 degrees. Place all ingredients in a large mixing bowl and stir vigorously until well combined. Lightly coat a 13- × 9-inch baking dish with cooking oil spray. Pour batter into baking dish and spread evenly. Bake for 20 to 25 minutes. Let cool before serving.

ESTIMATED PREPARATION TIME: 5 minutes.

ESTIMATED COOKING TIME: 20 minutes.

144 Calories
1.8 g Protein
27.8 g Carbohydrates
2.1 g Fat
1.0 g Fiber
126 mg Sodium
0 mg Cholesterol

Quick Applesauce Cake

Yield: 12 servings

Preheat oven to 375 degrees. Place dry cake mix in a large mixing bowl. Stir in baking powder and baking soda. Add egg substitute, water, and applesauce. Beat with an electric mixer on medium speed for 2 to 3 minutes until smooth.

Lightly coat a 13- × 9-inch baking pan with a cooking oil spray and pour batter into pan, spreading evenly. Bake for 25 to 30 minutes. Let cool before serving. Can be served plain or with a light sprinkling of powdered sugar.

- 1 package (18¼ ounces) spice cake mix
- 1 teaspoon baking powder
- ¼ teaspoon baking soda
- ¼ cup egg substitute
- ½ cup water
- 1 cup unsweetened applesauce

ESTIMATED PREPARATION TIME: 5 minutes.

ESTIMATED COOKING TIME: 25 minutes.

HIGH ALTITUDE NOTE: Omit baking soda and increase oven temperature to 400 degrees.

202 Calories
2.4 g Protein
38.3 g Carbohydrates
4.2 g Fat
1.1 g Fiber
310 mg Sodium
0 mg Cholesterol

Quick Banana-Blueberry Cake

Yield: 12 servings

1 package (18¼ ounces) yellow cake mix
¼ teaspoon baking soda
¼ cup egg substitute
½ cup water
1 medium banana, mashed
1 can (21 ounces) "lite" aspartame-sweetened blueberry pie filling

Preheat oven to 375 degrees. Place dry cake mix in a large mixing bowl. Stir in the baking soda. Add egg substitute, water, and banana. Beat with an electric mixer on medium speed for 2 to 3 minutes until smooth.

Lightly coat a 13- × 9-inch baking pan with cooking oil spray and pour batter into pan, spreading evenly. Spoon entire contents of canned blueberries onto cake batter and stir gently to distribute fruit evenly throughout batter. Bake for 25 to 30 minutes. Let cool before serving. Serve with a dollop of nonfat blueberry yogurt, if desired.

ESTIMATED PREPARATION TIME: 10 minutes.

ESTIMATED COOKING TIME: 25 minutes.

HIGH ALTITUDE NOTE: Omit baking soda and increase oven temperature to 400 degrees.

305 Calories
2.7 g Protein
68.3 g Carbohydrates
2.8 g Fat
0.9 g Fiber
352 mg Sodium
0 mg Cholesterol

Busy Mom's Lowfat Cookbook

Quick Black Forest Cake

Yield: 12 servings

Preheat oven to 375 degrees. Place dry cake mix in a large mixing bowl. Add egg substitute and water. Beat with an electric mixer on medium speed for 2 to 3 minutes until smooth.

Lightly coat a 13- × 9-inch baking pan with cooking oil spray and pour batter into pan, spreading evenly. Spoon entire contents of canned cherry pie filling onto cake batter and stir gently to distribute fruit evenly throughout batter. Bake for 25 to 30 minutes. Let cool before serving. Serve with a dollop of nondairy whipped topping for garnish.

1 package (18¼ ounces) chocolate cake mix
¼ cup egg substitute
½ cup water
1 can (21 ounces) "lite" cherry pie filling
nondairy whipped topping for garnish

ESTIMATED PREPARATION TIME: 10 minutes.

ESTIMATED COOKING TIME: 25 minutes.

HIGH ALTITUDE NOTE: Add 2 tablespoons flour to dry cake mix; increase oven temperature to 400 degrees.

226 Calories
2.4 g Protein
43.7 g Carbohydrates
4.7 g Fat
1.0 g Fiber
327 mg Sodium
0 mg Cholesterol

Quick Carrot Cake

Yield: 12 servings

1 package (18¼ ounces) spice cake mix
½ teaspoon baking powder
1 can (16 ounces) sliced carrots
¼ cup egg substitute
¼ cup water
½ cup raisins
Yogurt Cream for garnish (recipe follows)

Yogurt Cream
½ cup fat-free cream cheese, softened
½ cup nonfat plain yogurt
½ cup powdered sugar

Preheat oven to 375 degrees. Place dry cake mix in a large mixing bowl. Stir in the baking powder. Purée entire contents of canned carrots in blender or food processor. Add egg substitute, water, and puréed carrots to dry ingredients and beat with an electric mixer on medium speed for 2 to 3 minutes until smooth. Stir in raisins.

Lightly coat a 13- × 9-inch baking pan with cooking oil spray and pour batter into pan, spreading evenly. Bake for 25 to 30 minutes. Let cool before serving. Serve with Yogurt Cream for garnish.

For Yogurt Cream: Place all ingredients in a small bowl and beat with an electric mixer on medium speed for 2 to 3 minutes until smooth and creamy. Chill.

ESTIMATED PREPARATION TIME: 10 minutes.

ESTIMATED COOKING TIME: 25 minutes.

HIGH ALTITUDE NOTE: Omit baking soda and increase oven temperature to 400 degrees.

ESTIMATED PREPARATION TIME: 3 minutes for Yogurt Cream.

Cake/Yogurt Cream
220/29 Calories
2.8/1.8 g Protein
42.5/5.2 g Carbohydrates
4.3/0 g Fat
1.4/0 g Fiber
399/63 mg Sodium
0/2 mg Cholesterol

Busy Mom's Lowfat Cookbook

No-Bake Angel Food Cake

Yield: 12 servings

Prepare gelatin according to package instructions, and allow to cool slightly at room temperature. Arrange angel food cake cubes in the bottom of a 13- × 9-inch glass baking dish. Place frozen cherries in the baking dish, arranging them around and on top of the angel food cubes. Pour the slightly cooled gelatin over the cherries and cake. Chill for at least 2 hours. Serve with nondairy whipped topping.

2 packages (3 ounces each) aspartame-sweetened cherry gelatin mix
1 purchased angel food cake, cubed
1 package (16 ounces) frozen cherries
lowfat nondairy whipped topping for garnish

ESTIMATED PREPARATION TIME: 15 minutes.

226 Calories
4.7 g Protein
52.2 g Carbohydrates
0.4 g Fat
1.6 g Fiber
292 mg Sodium
0 mg Cholesterol

No-Bake Rocky Road Cake

Yield: 12 servings

1 purchased angel food cake, cubed
2 packages (3½ ounces each) chocolate pudding mix
3½ cups nonfat milk
½ cup dry-roasted peanuts, crushed or chopped
lowfat nondairy whipped topping

Line a 13- × 9-inch baking dish with waxed paper. Arrange angel food cubes in bottom of dish. Place pudding mix in a medium mixing bowl, add cold milk, and beat with an electric mixer on low speed until smooth. Stir in peanuts and pour the pudding mixture over the cake cubes. Chill for at least 2 hours. Serve with nondairy whipped topping.

ESTIMATED PREPARATION TIME: 15 minutes plus 2 hours chilling time.

252 Calories
7.4 g Protein
48.8 g Carbohydrates
3.8 g Fat
1.5 g Fiber
532 mg Sodium
1 mg Cholesterol

Busy Mom's Lowfat Cookbook

Quick Blackberry Cobbler

Yield: 12 servings

Preheat oven to 400 degrees. Place biscuit mix and sugar in a large mixing bowl and stir. Add egg substitute and water and stir vigorously for 1 to 2 minutes. Batter will be slightly lumpy.

Lightly coat a 13- × 9-inch baking dish with cooking oil spray. Pour batter into pan and sprinkle with frozen blackberries. Bake for 20 to 25 minutes. Let cool slightly and serve warm with nonfat frozen vanilla yogurt.

2 cups reduced-fat biscuit mix
2 tablespoons sugar
¼ cup egg substitute
¼ cup water
1 package (16 ounces) frozen blackberries

ESTIMATED PREPARATION TIME: 5 minutes.

ESTIMATED COOKING TIME: 20 minutes.

HIGH ALTITUDE NOTE: Increase oven temperature to 425 degrees.

99 Calories
2.1 g Protein
19.2 g Carbohydrates
1.5 g Fat
1.3 g Fiber
237 mg Sodium
0 mg Cholesterol

Quick Peach Cobbler

Yield: 12 servings

1 package (18¼ ounces) white cake mix
¼ teaspoon baking soda
½ cup nonfat plain yogurt
½ cup water
1 can (20 ounces) sliced peaches in light syrup

Preheat oven to 400 degrees. Place cake mix and baking soda in a large mixing bowl and stir. Add yogurt and water and stir vigorously for 1 to 2 minutes. Batter will be lumpy.

Lightly coat a 13- × 9-inch baking dish with cooking oil spray and pour batter into pan, spreading evenly. Drain ¼ cup of liquid from the canned peaches and discard. Pour the remaining contents of the canned peaches onto the batter, spreading evenly.

Bake for 20 to 25 minutes. Serve warm with nonfat frozen peach yogurt.

ESTIMATED PREPARATION TIME: 5 minutes.

ESTIMATED COOKING TIME: 20 minutes.

HIGH ALTITUDE NOTE: Omit the baking soda, add 2 tablespoons of flour, and increase oven temperature to 425 degrees.

215 Calories
2.8 g Protein
41.5 g Carbohydrates
4.2 g Fat
1.3 g Fiber
281 mg Sodium
0 mg Cholesterol

Quick Applesauce-Spice Bars

Yield: 32 cookie bars

Preheat oven to 375 degrees. Place all ingredients in a large mixing bowl and stir vigorously until well combined. Batter will be lumpy. Lightly coat a 13- × 9-inch baking pan with cooking oil spray and pour batter into pan, spreading evenly. Bake for 20 minutes. Allow to cool and dust with powdered sugar if desired. Cut into 3 × 1-inch bars.

1 package (18¼ ounces) spice cake mix
¼ cup reduced-fat margarine, softened
1 cup applesauce
1 whole egg or 2 egg whites
½ cup raisins

ESTIMATED PREPARATION TIME: 5 minutes.

ESTIMATED COOKING TIME: 20 minutes.

HIGH ALTITUDE NOTE: Increase oven temperature to 400 degrees.

93 Calories
1.0 g Protein
16.5 g Carbohydrates
2.6 g Fat
0.6 g Fiber
124 mg Sodium
6 mg Cholesterol

Easy Cherry Bars

Yield: 16 bars

1½ cups uncooked old-fashioned oats
1 cup reduced-fat biscuit mix
½ cup packed light brown sugar
¼ cup canola oil
¼ cup nonfat plain yogurt, at room temperature
1 can (21 ounces) "lite" cherry pie filling

Preheat oven to 400 degrees. Place oats, biscuit mix, and brown sugar in a large bowl. Add oil and yogurt and stir with a fork until evenly crumbly and evenly moist. Scoop out and set aside ½ cup of mixture for topping.

Line a 13- × 9-inch baking pan with aluminum foil and press remaining mixture evenly into the bottom of the baking pan. Spoon the cherry pie filling into the baking pan, spreading evenly. Sprinkle with reserved crumb mixture and bake for 15 to 20 minutes. Let cool before serving.

ESTIMATED PREPARATION TIME: 15 minutes.

ESTIMATED COOKING TIME: 15 minutes.

HIGH ALTITUDE NOTE: Increase oven temperature to 425 degrees.

150 Calories
2.0 g Protein
25.5 g Carbohydrates
4.5 g Fat
0.9 g Fiber
102 mg Sodium
0 mg Cholesterol

Busy Mom's Lowfat Cookbook

Quick Pumpkin-Walnut Bars

Yield: about 20 bars

Preheat oven to 400 degrees. Place dry cake mix and bran in a large mixing bowl and stir to combine. Add egg white, water, and canned pumpkin. Beat by hand, using a wooden spoon or stiff spatula, until well blended—about 2 minutes. Fold in chopped walnuts.

Lightly coat a 13- × 9-inch baking pan with cooking oil spray, and pour batter into pan, spreading evenly. Bake for 20 to 25 minutes. Allow to cool completely before cutting into 2-inch square bars.

1 package (18¼ ounces) spice cake mix
¼ cup wheat bran or crushed bran flakes
1 egg white, slightly beaten
⅓ cup water
1 cup canned pumpkin
½ cup chopped walnuts

ESTIMATED PREPARATION TIME: 5 minutes.

ESTIMATED COOKING TIME: 20 minutes.

HIGH ALTITUDE NOTE: Increase oven temperature to 425 degrees.

143 Calories
2.1 g Protein
23.8 g Carbohydrates
4.6 g Fat
1.2 g Fiber
172 mg Sodium
0 mg Cholesterol

Bring On Dessert!

Chocolate Chip Bar Cookies

Yield: about 3 dozen bar cookies

1 package (18¼ ounces)
   white cake mix
⅓ cup reduced-fat
   margarine
⅓ cup nonfat sour cream
2 egg whites
½ cup chopped pecans
1 package (16 ounces)
   chocolate chips

Preheat oven to 375 degrees. Place 1 cup of the cake mix and the margarine, sour cream, and egg whites in a large bowl and cream together. Gradually stir in remaining cake mix. Stir in chopped nuts and chocolate chips. Spread dough on a nonstick cookie sheet and bake for 15 minutes or until lightly browned. Let cool before cutting into 1- × 3-inch bars.

ESTIMATED PREPARATION TIME: 10 minutes.

ESTIMATED COOKING TIME: 15 minutes.

HIGH ALTITUDE NOTE: Increase oven temperature to 400 degrees.

144 Calories
1.6 g Protein
19.3 g Carbohydrates
7.6 g Fat
0.6 g Fiber
110 mg Sodium
0 mg Cholesterol

Busy Mom's Lowfat Cookbook

Quick Carrot-Raisin Cookies

Yield: about 4 dozen cookies

Preheat oven to 375 degrees. Place cake mix, egg substitute, margarine, and carrots in a large mixing bowl and beat vigorously by hand until well combined. Stir in raisins. Drop by teaspoonfuls, about 2 inches apart, on a nonstick cookie sheet. Sprinkle with coconut and bake for 10 to 12 minutes. Let cool before serving.

ESTIMATED PREPARATION TIME: 10 minutes.

ESTIMATED COOKING TIME: 20 to 30 minutes.

HIGH ALTITUDE NOTE: Increase oven temperature to 400 degrees.

1 package (18¼ ounces) carrot cake mix
¼ cup egg substitute
¼ cup reduced-fat margarine, softened
1 jar (4 ounces) puréed carrots (baby food)
½ cup raisins
⅓ cup shredded coconut

56 Calories
0.7 g Protein
9.8 g Carbohydrates
1.8 g Fat
0.5 g Fiber
74 mg Sodium
0 mg Cholesterol

Quick Gingerbread Drop Cookies

Yield: about 3 dozen cookies

1 package (14½ ounces)
  gingerbread mix
½ cup water
1 cup raisins
½ cup chopped nuts

Preheat oven to 375 degrees. Place gingerbread mix in a large mixing bowl, add water, and stir vigorously to blend well. Fold in raisins and nuts. Drop by teaspoonfuls, about 2 inches apart, on a nonstick cookie sheet and bake for 10 to 12 minutes. Let cool before serving.

ESTIMATED PREPARATION TIME: 5 minutes.

ESTIMATED COOKING TIME: 20 to 30 minutes.

HIGH ALTITUDE NOTE: Increase oven temperature to 400 degrees.

73 Calories
0.9 g Protein
12.2 g Carbohydrates
2.6 g Fat
0.7 g Fiber
75 mg Sodium
0 mg Cholesterol

Quick Peanut Butter Cookies

Yield: about 4 dozen cookies

Preheat oven to 375 degrees. Place peanut butter, water, and egg substitute in a large bowl. Add 1 cup of the cake mix and beat until smooth. Gradually add remaining cake mix. Drop dough by teaspoonfuls, about 2 inches apart, on a nonstick cookie sheet. Bake for 8 to 10 minutes. Allow to cool slightly before removing from cookie sheet.

1 cup reduced-fat peanut
  butter
⅓ cup water
¼ cup egg substitute
1 package (18¼ ounces)
  yellow cake mix

ESTIMATED PREPARATION TIME: 10 minutes.

ESTIMATED COOKING TIME: 20 to 35 minutes.

HIGH ALTITUDE NOTE: Increase oven temperature to
400 degrees.

75 Calories
2.1 g Protein
11.2 g Carbohydrates
2.7 g Fat
0.5 g Fiber
106 mg Sodium
0 mg Cholesterol

PBJ Cookie Treats

Yield: about 3 dozen cookies

¼ cup light brown sugar, packed
¼ cup granulated sugar
½ cup reduced-fat peanut butter
¼ cup plain lowfat yogurt
1 egg
1 cup all-purpose flour
1 tablespoon wheat germ
1 teaspoon baking soda
⅔ cup quick-cooking oatmeal
All-fruit spread

Preheat oven to 375 degrees. Cream together sugars, peanut butter, yogurt, and egg. In a small bowl, stir together flour, wheat germ, and baking soda. Add to creamed sugar mixture and blend well.

Form dough into 1-inch balls, and roll in the oats before placing on a nonstick cookie sheet. Using your thumb, make a dent in each cookie. Bake for 10 to 12 minutes, or until lightly browned. Remove from oven and cool.

When cool, place a dollop of fruit spread in the thumbprint.

ESTIMATED PREPARATION TIME: 15 minutes.

ESTIMATED COOKING TIME: 20 to 30 minutes.

HIGH ALTITUDE NOTE: Increase oven temperature to 400 degrees.

65 Calories
2.0 g Protein
10.6 g Carbohydrates
1.6 g Fat
0.5 g Fiber
60 mg Sodium
6 mg Cholesterol

Busy Mom's Lowfat Cookbook

Banana Split Pie

Yield: 6 to 8 servings

Slice one banana and arrange slices in the bottom of the pie shell. Prepare chocolate pudding according to the package directions, using 2 cups of the milk. Pour over the bananas in the pie shell. Slice the second banana and arrange slices on the chocolate pudding. Prepare vanilla pudding according to the package directions, using 2 cups of the milk. Pour over bananas in the pie shell. Chill for at least 4 hours. Slice and garnish with nondairy whipped topping and chocolate syrup, if desired.

2 medium bananas
1 prepared graham cracker pie shell
1 package (3½ ounces) fat-free chocolate pudding mix
1 package (3½ ounces) fat-free vanilla pudding mix
4 cups skim milk reduced-fat nondairy whipped topping

ESTIMATED PREPARATION TIME: 15 minutes plus 4 hours chilling time.

308 Calories
5.9 g Protein
54.8 g Carbohydrates
7.6 g Fat
2.5 g Fiber
640 mg Sodium
2 mg Cholesterol

Chapter 9

Guess Who's Coming to Dinner?

My family has always been hospitable, and anyone is welcome to join us for dinner any time. Of course, this means that there are sometimes last-minute dinner guests, and my planned menu won't suffice.

Whether your kitchen has a lot of visitors (as mine does), or someone just popped in close to dinnertime, unexpected company can leave you scrambling for ideas. You may not be thinking "gourmet," but chances are you'd like to make the meal a little special.

A few pantry items are all you need to whip up something quick, delicious, and healthy. The following recipes supply ample servings to feed a small crowd. I've included recipes for main dishes, quick breads, salads, beverages, and after-dinner treats. You can also use recipes from other sections of this book and customize a menu to suit your taste and food supply.

Shh! Vegetable Meat Loaf

Yield: 10 to 12 servings

Preheat oven to 425 degrees. Purée vegetables in blender or food processor. Place all ingredients in a large mixing bowl and mix until well combined and stiff. Lightly coat a glass loaf pan with cooking oil spray. Form meat mixture into a loaf and place in pan.

Microwave on Medium High for 12 minutes, turning once at 6 minutes. Remove from microwave oven and bake in regular oven for 10 minutes or until lightly browned. Serve with mashed potatoes and salad.

1 can (16 ounces) mixed
  vegetables, drained
1 pound extra-lean
  ground beef
2 tablespoons catsup
1 teaspoon dehydrated
  minced onion
1 teaspoon soy sauce
1 egg white
½ cup quick-cooking oats
½ cup crushed corn flakes
¼ cup wheat germ

ESTIMATED PREPARATION TIME: 10 minutes.

ESTIMATED COOKING TIME: 22 minutes.

140 Calories
10.7 g Protein
10.9 g Carbohydrates
6.0 g Fat
1.2 g Fiber
177 mg Sodium
27 mg Cholesterol

Quick Sloppy Joes

Yield: 8 servings

1½ pounds ground chuck
½ cup chopped onion
½ cup catsup
¼ cup spicy steak sauce
1 tablespoon sweet pickle
   relish
8 whole wheat buns

In a medium nonstick pot, brown the ground chuck and onions over medium-high heat. Drain excess fat. Add the catsup, steak sauce, and relish. Reduce heat and simmer, stirring occasionally, until sauce is heated through. Serve on buns with lettuce and tomato, if desired.

ESTIMATED PREPARATION TIME: 2 minutes.

ESTIMATED COOKING TIME: 10 to 15 minutes.

309 Calories
21.9 g Protein
24.3 g Carbohydrates
13.6 g Fat
3.4 g Fiber
570 mg Sodium
57 mg Cholesterol

Busy Mom's Lowfat Cookbook

Midwestern Beans

Yield: 12 servings

Preheat oven to 375 degrees. Place ground beef, bacon, and onion in a large nonstick skillet and brown over medium-high heat. Carefully drain excess fat, and pat dry with paper towels to absorb additional fat. Place all the beans in a large casserole dish and add the browned meat and onions. Add catsup, dry mustard, vinegar, and sugar, and mix well to combine. Cover and bake for 30 minutes.

ESTIMATED PREPARATION TIME: 15 minutes.

ESTIMATED COOKING TIME: 30 minutes.

1 pound lean ground beef
½ pound bacon, diced
1 cup chopped onion
2 cans (16 ounces each) pork and beans
1 can (16 ounces) kidney beans, drained
1 can (16 ounces) lima beans, drained
1½ cups catsup
1 teaspoon dry mustard
2 tablespoons vinegar
¾ cup brown sugar

351 Calories
18.8 g Protein
50.1 g Carbohydrates
9.7 g Fat
7.1 g Fiber
1052 mg Sodium
40 mg Cholesterol

Grilled Cranberry Pork Chops

Yield: 6 servings

1 can (8 ounces) smooth
   cranberry sauce
2 teaspoons lemon juice
½ teaspoon cinnamon
⅛ teaspoon ginger
6 pork chops, trimmed
   (about 2 to 2½
   pounds)

Light charcoal in a grill. Place cranberry sauce, lemon juice, cinnamon, and ginger in a microwavable dish and microwave on High for 1 minute. Stir and microwave on High for an additional minute. Stir again and set aside.

When coals are medium hot, place pork chops on grill and brush with sauce. Grill for 8 minutes, occasionally brushing with sauce. Turn the chops and grill for an additional 5 minutes, or until done, continuing to occasionally brush with the sauce. Remove from grill, discard any remaining sauce, and serve.

ESTIMATED PREPARATION TIME: 5 minutes.

ESTIMATED COOKING TIME: 13 minutes.

386 Calories
27.3 g Protein
18.6 g Carbohydrates
22.0 g Fat
0.2 g Fiber
83 mg Sodium
96 mg Cholesterol

Busy Mom's Lowfat Cookbook

Sausage and Beer Stew

Yield: 8 servings

Place all ingredients in a large nonstick stock pot. Heat to boiling over medium-high heat, stirring occasionally. Reduce to low heat, cover, and simmer for 20 minutes. Using a slotted spoon, transfer stew to a large serving bowl.

ESTIMATED PREPARATION TIME: 10 minutes.

ESTIMATED COOKING TIME: 30 minutes.

1 pound reduced-fat kielbasa (Polish sausage) or smoked sausage, cut into 1-inch pieces
8 small new potatoes, washed and halved
1 package (16 ounces) fresh baby carrots
1 can or bottle (12 ounces) beer
½ cup water
2 teaspoons beef bouillon granules (or 2 cubes)
⅛ teaspoon thyme
⅛ teaspoon basil
½ teaspoon minced garlic
1 teaspoon minced onion

167 Calories
12.7 g Protein
25.2 g Carbohydrates
1.2 g Fat
2.3 g Fiber
871 mg Sodium
15 mg Cholesterol

Grilled Sausage and Vegetables

Yield: 6 complete servings

6 ears corn
6 russet potatoes
3 zucchini
1 pound reduced-fat
     kielbasa (Polish
     sausage)
  Herb Butter (see recipe
     below)

Herb Butter
½ cup reduced-fat
     margarine, softened
1 tablespoon chopped
     fresh basil
½ teaspoon garlic salt

Light charcoal in a grill. Wash vegetables, but leave corn in the husks. Cut potatoes in half lengthwise, and leave in skins. When coals are hot, arrange corn and potatoes (face down) on grill, cover, and cook for 15 minutes.

Trim stems from zucchini and slice in half lengthwise. Rearrange corn and potatoes on grill, and place sausage and zucchini in hottest part of the grill. Cover and roast for 5 minutes. Turn the meat and vegetables, turning potatoes face up. Cover and roast for an additional 5 minutes. Remove all food from grill.

Using oven mitts, carefully remove husk from corn and snap each ear in half. Slice the sausage diagonally into 6 pieces. Serve with Herb Butter for vegetables.

For Herb Butter: Vigorously stir all ingredients with a fork in a small bowl until well combined. Chill.

Grilled items/Herb Butter
395/67 Calories
21.0/0 g Protein
75.9/0.1 g Carbohydrates
2.6/7.6 g Fat
6.3/0 g Fiber
842/348 mg Sodium
20/0 mg Cholesterol

ESTIMATED PREPARATION TIME: 10 minutes.

ESTIMATED COOKING TIME: 25 minutes.

Busy Mom's Lowfat Cookbook

Last-Minute Lasagna

Yield: 12 generous servings

Preheat oven to 400 degrees. Lightly coat a 13- × 9-inch cake pan with cooking oil spray.

Drizzle ½ cup of spaghetti sauce in the bottom of the pan. Arrange uncooked lasagna noodles on top of this to fill the bottom of the pan (about 3 noodles). Spoon ⅔ cup of the cottage cheese onto the noodles, spreading it out. Add one-third of the broccoli. Sprinkle with ½ cup mozzarella cheese. Place another layer of lasagna noodles on top.

In a large bowl, combine tomatoes and remaining spaghetti sauce. Spoon sauce generously over noodles.

Begin again by layering cottage cheese, broccoli, and mozzarella. Top with another layer of noodles. Spoon more sauce over noodles and repeat layering a third time.

Top the final layer of noodles with the remainder of the sauce. Sprinkle with bread crumbs, remaining mozzarella, and Parmesan cheese. Cover with foil, and bake for 30 minutes. Remove foil and bake 5 minutes more, or until the top is lightly browned. Serve hot with garlic bread and salad.

ESTIMATED PREPARATION TIME: 15 minutes.

ESTIMATED COOKING TIME: 35 minutes.

1 can or jar (26 ounces) prepared spaghetti sauce
1 package (16 ounces) lasagna noodles
2 cups nonfat cottage cheese
1 package (16 ounces) frozen chopped broccoli, thawed
1½ cups reduced-fat shredded mozzarella cheese
2 cans (16 ounces each) diced tomatoes
⅓ cup plain bread crumbs
¼ cup reduced-fat grated Parmesan cheese

318 Calories
16.9 g Protein
48.5 g Carbohydrates
7.0 g Fat
2.9 g Fiber
720 mg Sodium
11 mg Cholesterol

Guess Who's Coming to Dinner?

185

Easy Macaroni and Cheese Bake

Yield: 12 servings

⅓ cup reduced-fat margarine, sliced into pats and chilled

2 cups elbow macaroni, uncooked

1 can (12 ounces) evaporated skim milk

1 cup skim milk

½ cup egg substitute

¼ teaspoon salt

¼ teaspoon pepper

2 cups shredded fat-free Cheddar cheese

Preheat oven to 400 degrees. Arrange margarine in the bottom of a 13- × 9-inch baking pan. Sprinkle macaroni evenly over margarine. In a medium bowl, beat together the evaporated skim milk, skim milk, egg substitute, salt, and pepper. Pour mixture over macaroni and sprinkle evenly with the cheese. Cover the baking dish with foil and bake for 25 minutes. Remove foil and bake for an additional 2 to 3 minutes to brown.

ESTIMATED PREPARATION TIME: 5 minutes.

ESTIMATED COOKING TIME: 27 minutes.

152 Calories
10.3 g Protein
20.9 g Carbohydrates
3.2 g Fat
0.5 g Fiber
302 mg Sodium
2 mg Cholesterol

Busy Mom's Lowfat Cookbook

Simply Minestrone

Yield: 6 to 8 servings

Empty entire contents of all canned vegetables into a large nonstick stock pot. Add water, bouillon, and Italian seasoning. Bring to a low boil over medium-high heat, then stir in the pasta. Reduce heat to low, cover, and simmer for 8 minutes, or until pasta is tender.

ESTIMATED PREPARATION TIME: 2 minutes.

ESTIMATED COOKING TIME: 15 minutes.

1 can (15 ounces) diced tomatoes
1 can (16 ounces) mixed vegetables
1 can (16 ounces) pork and beans
1 cup water
2 teaspoons beef bouillon granules (or 2 cubes)
½ teaspoon Italian seasoning herb mix
1 cup uncooked pasta shells or rings

138 Calories
6.4 g Protein
27.6 g Carbohydrates
1.1 g Fat
4.5 g Fiber
697 mg Sodium
4 mg Cholesterol

Quick Cheese Biscuits

Yield: 10 biscuits

1 can (7½ ounces)
  refrigerated biscuits
¼ cup reduced-fat
  shredded Cheddar
  cheese

Preheat oven according to biscuit package instructions. Assemble biscuits in an 8-inch round nonstick cake pan. Sprinkle with cheese and bake as directed.

ESTIMATED PREPARATION TIME: 2 minutes.

ESTIMATED COOKING TIME: 10 minutes.

67 Calories
2.3 g Protein
11.1 g Carbohydrates
1.5 g Fat
0 g Fiber
308 mg Sodium
2 mg Cholesterol

Easy Herbed Rolls

Yield: about 1 dozen rolls

Dissolve yeast and 1 tablespoon of the sugar in warm water. Place potato flakes, remaining sugar, oil, egg white, salt, and thyme in a large mixing bowl. Pour in yeast mixture and stir. Add ½ cup of the flour and mix until smooth, then gradually add remaining flour until a stiff dough is formed. Transfer dough to a lightly floured work surface and gently knead until smooth and elastic. Allow dough to rest for 5 minutes.

Tear off bits of dough and form into 2-inch balls. Place on nonstick cookie sheet about 2 inches apart. Allow to rise until doubled in size (30 minutes to 1 hour). Bake in preheated 400-degree oven for 15 minutes.

1 package fast-rising yeast
⅓ cup sugar
½ cup warm water
½ cup instant mashed potato flakes
⅓ cup canola oil
1 egg white, slightly beaten
½ teaspoon salt
1 teaspoon thyme or crushed basil
3 cups flour

ESTIMATED PREPARATION TIME: 15 minutes plus rising time.

ESTIMATED COOKING TIME: 15 minutes.

198 Calories
3.9 g Protein
30.8 g Carbohydrates
6.5 g Fat
0.9 g Fiber
97 mg Sodium
0 mg Cholesterol

New-Fashioned Bread Pudding

Yield: 8 servings

4 cups fresh bread
   crumbs
1¾ cups skim milk
¼ cup canola oil
1 teaspoon salt
½ cup egg substitute
¼ teaspoon cinnamon
1 teaspoon vanilla
1 cup raisins

Preheat oven to 375 degrees. Lightly coat a 1½-quart baking dish with cooking oil spray, and place bread crumbs in dish. Heat milk and oil in a small saucepan to lukewarm, then add the salt, egg substitute, cinnamon, vanilla, and raisins. Pour over bread crumbs and stir lightly. Place dish in a larger baking pan and place in oven. Pour hot water into larger dish until filled to a depth of about 1 inch. Bake for 30 minutes or until soft and firm.

ESTIMATED PREPARATION TIME: 10 minutes.

ESTIMATED COOKING TIME: 30 minutes.

207 Calories
5.7 g Protein
28.9 g Carbohydrates
8.4 g Fat
3.0 g Fiber
431 mg Sodium
1 mg Cholesterol

Fast Three-Bean Salad

Yield: 8 servings

Place beans and pimientos in a large bowl. In a small bowl, combine vinegar, honey, onion, and parsley, stirring until honey is completely dissolved. Pour over beans, toss gently, cover, and chill.

ESTIMATED PREPARATION TIME: 10 minutes.

1 can (16 ounces) green beans, drained
1 can (16 ounces) garbanzo beans, drained
1 can (16 ounces) kidney beans, drained
1 jar (2 ounces) pimiento, drained
¼ cup white wine vinegar
2 tablespoons honey
1 teaspoon dehydrated minced onion
1 teaspoon parsley flakes

108 Calories
4.7 g Protein
22.0 g Carbohydrates
0.7 g Fat
3.9 g Fiber
245 mg Sodium
0 mg Cholesterol

Broccoli Deluxe

Yield: 12 servings

3 packages (10 ounces each) frozen chopped broccoli, thawed
1 can (15¾ ounces) cream of mushroom soup
¼ cup light olive oil
¼ cup egg substitute
3 tablespoons chopped onion
1 cup reduced-fat shredded Cheddar cheese
1 cup crushed saltine crackers

Preheat oven to 350 degrees. In a large bowl, combine broccoli, soup, oil, egg substitute, onion, and ¾ cup of the Cheddar cheese, then transfer mixture to a large casserole dish. Sprinkle remaining ¼ cup Cheddar cheese and crushed saltines on top of mixture. Bake, uncovered, for 20 minutes.

ESTIMATED PREPARATION TIME: 5 minutes.

ESTIMATED COOKING TIME: 20 minutes.

147 Calories
6.0 g Protein
12.0 g Carbohydrates
8.8 g Fat
1.8 g Fiber
410 mg Sodium
10 mg Cholesterol

Busy Mom's Lowfat Cookbook

Calico Cabbage

Yield: 12 servings

Preheat oven to 375 degrees. Lightly coat a large casserole dish with cooking oil spray. Place vegetables in casserole, then sprinkle with sugar, salt, and pepper. Arrange pats of margarine on top. Cover and bake for 30 minutes, or until cabbage is tender.

ESTIMATED PREPARATION TIME: 15 minutes.

ESTIMATED COOKING TIME: 30 minutes.

1 small head cabbage, chopped
4 carrots, shredded
½ cup chopped onion
½ cup chopped celery
¼ cup sugar
1 teaspoon salt
¼ teaspoon pepper
¼ cup reduced-fat margarine, sliced into pats

111 Calories
2.2 g Protein
22.0 g Carbohydrates
2.5 g Fat
5.8 g Fiber
284 mg Sodium
0 mg Cholesterol

Easy Succotash

Yield: 8 servings

1 can (15 ounces) lima or butter beans, drained
1 can (15 ounces) whole-kernel corn, drained
3 tablespoons mild salsa
1 tablespoon reduced-fat margarine
¼ teaspoon dried chives

Place beans, corn, salsa, and margarine in a medium saucepan. Heat over medium-low heat, stirring occasionally, until heated through and margarine has melted. Sprinkle with chives and serve.

ESTIMATED PREPARATION TIME: 3 minutes.

ESTIMATED COOKING TIME: 10 minutes.

272 Calories
15.4 g Protein
51.6 g Carbohydrates
1.7 g Fat
4.8 g Fiber
1129 mg Sodium
0 mg Cholesterol

Busy Mom's Lowfat Cookbook

Southern Stewed Tomatoes

Yield: 10 servings

Place entire contents of canned tomatoes, margarine, sugar, cinnamon, and salt in a medium nonstick pot and bring to a boil over medium heat, stirring frequently. In a small bowl, whisk together flour and water until smooth. Stirring constantly, gradually pour into tomatoes and simmer until thickened to desired consistency.

1 can (21 ounces) peeled tomatoes
¼ cup reduced-fat margarine
¼ cup sugar
¼ teaspoon cinnamon
¼ teaspoon salt
1 tablespoon flour
¼ cup water

ESTIMATED PREPARATION TIME: 2 minutes.

ESTIMATED COOKING TIME: 15 minutes.

52 Calories
0.7 g Protein
7.6 g Carbohydrates
2.4 g Fat
0.3 g Fiber
210 mg Sodium
0 mg Cholesterol

Banana Cream Pie

Yield: 6 to 8 servings

1 package (3½ ounces)
   fat-free vanilla
   pudding mix
2 cups cold skim milk
1 banana
1 cup miniature
   marshmallows
1 prepared graham
   cracker pie crust

Prepare vanilla pudding according to package directions, using 2 cups of milk. Slice banana and add to pudding along with marshmallows, folding in gently. Pour
pudding mixture into pie shell and refrigerate for at
least 2 hours.

ESTIMATED PREPARATION TIME: 10 minutes plus
                              refrigeration time.

336 Calories
4.9 g Protein
64.4 g Carbohydrates
7.9 g Fat
3.8 g Fiber
400 mg Sodium
1 mg Cholesterol

Busy Mom's Lowfat Cookbook

No-Bake Peach Pie

Yield: 6 to 8 servings

Arrange peach slices in the bottom of the pie shell. Dissolve gelatin in the boiling water. Place frozen yogurt in a medium bowl. Pour gelatin over frozen yogurt and stir until yogurt is completely melted and gelatin is mixed well. Pour over peaches, then place in freezer for 1½ to 2 hours.

ESTIMATED PREPARATION TIME: 10 minutes plus freezing time.

1 prepared graham cracker pie crust
1 can (21 ounces) sliced peaches, drained
1 package (3 ounces) peach-flavored gelatin
1 cup boiling water
1 cup nonfat frozen vanilla yogurt

222 Calories
3.2 g Protein
36.9 g Carbohydrates
7.5 g Fat
2.6 g Fiber
226 mg Sodium
2 mg Cholesterol

Fruited Ambrosia

Yield: 12 servings

1 can (20 ounces) fruit
    cocktail in juice,
    drained
1 cup sliced strawberries
1 banana, sliced
1 cup miniature
    marshmallows
½ cup chopped dry
    roasted nuts
¼ cup shredded coconut
½ cup fat-free sour cream
½ cup powdered sugar

Mix all ingredients thoroughly in a large bowl. Cover and chill.

ESTIMATED PREPARATION TIME: **10 minutes.**

100 Calories
2.2 g Protein
16.3 g Carbohydrates
3.6 g Fat
1.3 g Fiber
14 mg Sodium
0 mg Cholesterol

Chapter 10

Festive Foods for Family Celebrations

No-Bake Pumpkin
Cheese Pie

Potato Latkes

Lower-Fat Lekach

Quick Cinnamon Rolls

Easy Holiday Ham
Dinner

Light Green Bean
Casserole

Chocolate Puff Cookies

Easy Holiday Cookies

Quick Mincemeat
Turnovers

Hamantaschen

Passover Matzo Layer
Cake

Orange Chicken (Kosher)

Sugar-and-Cinnamon
Passover Cookies
(Kosher)

Sunny Orange Rolls

Easter Raspberry
Cheesecake

Easy Rack-of-Lamb
Dinner

Easy Hot Cross Buns

Independence Cake

Grilled Buffalo Burgers

Summer Pasta Salad

Holidays. Sometimes we love them, and sometimes we dread them. As a busy, working mom, I can't always reproduce the holiday meals my own mother spent hours preparing. I'd rather be *making* memories than baking memories.

Aside from the time it takes to prepare heirloom recipes, the rich foods can increase grocery bills and waistlines—neither of which sparks a festive spirit. This section includes recipes for traditional fare with a streamlined touch. I've included items for Hanukkah, Christmas, Passover, and Easter. I've also included a few fun recipes for less well known holidays, such as hamantaschen (three-sided filled cookies) for Purim, as well as a few recipes for an afternoon tea party.

For more easy holiday recipe ideas, see the Crock-Pot and dessert chapters of this cookbook, and be sure to check out the soup chapter for those days when you've shopped till you dropped and you still have a dinner to prepare.

Holidays are meant to be enjoyed. Invite your family to join you in the kitchen, and have fun before, during, and after your holiday meals.

No-Bake Pumpkin Cheese Pie

Yield: 6 to 8 servings

Sprinkle gelatin over water in a small bowl and let stand for 1 minute. Stir gently to dissolve and set aside. Place cream cheese, pumpkin, sugar, and spice in a large mixing bowl. Beat at low speed with an electric mixer until well combined. Gradually add gelatin mixture, beating on medium-low speed until mixture is creamy. Pour into pie shell and chill for at least 4 hours.

ESTIMATED PREPARATION TIME: 15 minutes plus 4 hours chilling time.

1 envelope unflavored gelatin
¼ cup very hot tap water
1 cup fat-free cream cheese, softened
1 cup canned pumpkin
1 cup granulated brown sugar
1 teaspoon pumpkin pie spice
1 prepared graham cracker pie shell

288 Calories
6.4 g Protein
49.2 g Carbohydrates
7.3 g Fat
2.3 g Fiber
373 mg Sodium
5 mg Cholesterol

Potato Latkes

Yield: 24 latkes

4 russet potatoes, peeled
   and shredded
¾ cup finely chopped
   onion
¼ cup flour
1 teaspoon salt
¼ teaspoon pepper
¼ cup egg substitute
1 teaspoon canola oil

Preheat oven to 450 degrees. Place potatoes, onion, flour, salt, and pepper into a large bowl. Toss well to evenly coat potatoes with flour and seasonings. Add the egg substitute and oil, and toss to coat potatoes evenly.

Lightly coat a nonstick cookie sheet with cooking oil spray and drop rounded teaspoonfuls of the potato mixture onto the cookie sheet. Press lightly to flatten. Bake for 10 minutes. Carefully turn latkes, change position of the cookie sheets, and bake an additional 5 minutes.

ESTIMATED PREPARATION TIME: 20 minutes.

ESTIMATED COOKING TIME: 15 minutes.

24 Calories
0.7 g Protein
4.4 g Carbohydrates
0.4 g Fat
0.3 g Fiber
94 mg Sodium
0 mg Cholesterol

Busy Mom's Lowfat Cookbook

Lower-Fat Lekach

Yield: 12 servings

Preheat oven to 375 degrees. Place the margarine, egg substitute, and sugar in a large mixing bowl and beat well. Stir in honey and coffee. In a separate bowl, combine flours, baking powder, baking soda, and spice. Add dry ingredients to the egg mixture and beat well. Stir in almond slivers. Lightly coat a 13- × 9-inch baking pan with cooking oil spray and cover bottom with waxed paper. Pour mixture into baking pan and bake for 40 to 50 minutes. Allow to cool before serving.

2 tablespoons reduced-fat margarine, softened
½ cup egg substitute
1 cup sugar
1 cup honey
1 cup strong black coffee
1½ cups whole wheat flour
1½ cups cake flour
1½ teaspoons baking powder
1 teaspoon baking soda
2 teaspoons pumpkin pie spice
½ cup slivered almonds

ESTIMATED PREPARATION TIME: 10 minutes.

ESTIMATED COOKING TIME: 45 minutes.

HIGH ALTITUDE NOTE: Not recommended for high altitudes.

294 Calories
5.3 g Protein
62.4 g Carbohydrates
3.9 g Fat
3.0 g Fiber
173 mg Sodium
0 mg Cholesterol

Festive Foods for Family Celebrations

203

Quick Cinnamon Rolls

Yield: 12 rolls

1¾ cups flour
¼ cup whole wheat flour
¼ cup sugar
2 teaspoons baking
   powder
½ teaspoon baking soda
⅓ cup reduced-fat
   margarine
¾ cup skim milk
   butter-flavored oil spray
1 cup packed light brown
   sugar
2 teaspoons cinnamon

Powdered Sugar Icing
1 cup powdered sugar
2 tablespoons skim milk

Preheat oven to 450 degrees. Place both flours, sugar, baking powder, and baking soda in a large mixing bowl and stir. Using a pastry blender or a fork, cut in margarine until the mixture resembles bread crumbs. Stir in milk ¼ cup at a time until the dough is stiff and begins to form a ball. If the dough becomes too sticky, work in more flour, 1 tablespoon at a time. Transfer dough to a floured work surface. Knead gently until dough is elastic (approximately 1 minute). Roll out to ¼ inch thick. Coat the dough with butter-flavored cooking oil spray. In a small bowl, stir together the brown sugar and cinnamon, then sprinkle over dough. Roll the dough tightly to form a tube, then slice into 1-inch rounds. Arrange side by side on a nonstick cookie sheet and bake for 10 minutes. Allow to cool and spread tops with Powdered Sugar Icing, if desired.

For Powdered Sugar Icing: Place sugar in a small bowl, add milk, and stir vigorously until smooth.

ESTIMATED PREPARATION TIME: 20 minutes.

ESTIMATED COOKING TIME: 10 minutes.

Cinnamon Rolls with Icing
220 Calories
2.5 g Protein
46.5 g Carbohydrates
2.9 g Fat
0.6 g Fiber
325 mg Sodium
0 mg Cholesterol

Busy Mom's Lowfat Cookbook

Easy Holiday Ham Dinner

Yield: 8 servings

Preheat oven to 350 degrees. Score the top of the ham and stud with cloves. Place ham in roasting pan. Drain pineapple, reserving the liquid, and lay pineapple slices on top of ham. Place a maraschino cherry in the center of each pineapple slice, using toothpicks to secure. Drain yams, reserving the liquid, and arrange around ham in roasting pan. Combine pineapple juice and yam syrup in a small bowl, and blend in brown sugar. Pour over ham and yams. Cover and bake for 30 minutes.

3-pound lean turkey ham
1 tablespoon whole cloves
1 can (15 ounces) pineapple rings, in juice
5 or 6 maraschino cherries
1 can (15 ounces) yams
¼ cup packed brown sugar

ESTIMATED PREPARATION TIME: 10 minutes.

ESTIMATED COOKING TIME: 30 minutes.

241 Calories
16.3 g Protein
33.3 g Carbohydrates
4.6 g Fat
1.6 g Fiber
863 mg Sodium
108 mg Cholesterol

Light Green Bean Casserole

Yield: 8 servings

2 cans (16 ounces each)
    green beans, drained
1 cup nonfat sour cream
1 teaspoon lemon juice
1 teaspoon lemon zest
¼ teaspoon pepper
1 teaspoon cornstarch
½ of a 16-ounce package
    frozen onion rings

Preheat oven to 350 degrees. Lightly coat a casserole dish with cooking oil spray and place green beans in dish. Place sour cream, lemon juice, lemon zest, pepper, and cornstarch in a small bowl, blend, and pour over green beans. Assemble frozen onion rings on top of green beans and bake uncovered for 20 minutes, or until onion rings are lightly browned.

ESTIMATED PREPARATION TIME: 10 minutes.

ESTIMATED COOKING TIME: 20 minutes.

146 Calories
4.4 g Protein
16.6 g Carbohydrates
7.7 g Fat
1.1 g Fiber
317 mg Sodium
0 mg Cholesterol

Busy Mom's Lowfat Cookbook

Chocolate Puff Cookies

Yield: about 3 dozen cookies

Preheat oven to 375 degrees. Place frosting and egg whites in a large mixing bowl and cream with electric mixer. In a separate bowl, combine flour, salt, and baking soda. Add flour mixture to frosting mixture, one-third at a time, blending well with a wooden spoon. Dough should be slightly stiff. Scoop teaspoonfuls of dough and roll into balls. Arrange balls on a nonstick cookie sheet about 3 inches apart. Bake for 8 to 10 minutes.

1 tub (16 ounces) reduced-fat prepared chocolate frosting
2 egg whites
2 cups flour
½ teaspoon salt
1 teaspoon baking soda

ESTIMATED PREPARATION TIME: 10 minutes.

ESTIMATED COOKING TIME: 16 to 24 minutes.

HIGH ALTITUDE NOTE: Reduce baking soda to ½ teaspoon and increase oven temperature to 400 degrees.

76 Calories
1.1 g Protein
13.4 g Carbohydrates
2.0 g Fat
0.2 g Fiber
76 mg Sodium
0 mg Cholesterol

Easy Holiday Cookies

Yield: about 4 dozen cookies

1 package (20 ounces) reduced-fat refrigerated sugar cookie dough
1 cup chopped pecans
1 jar (10 ounces) maraschino cherry halves, drained

Place cookie dough in freezer for 1 hour before preparing. Preheat oven to 375 degrees. Slice the cookie dough into 1-inch segments, and quarter. Form dough quarters into balls, roll in chopped nuts, and place on a nonstick cookie sheet about 3 inches apart. Press a maraschino cherry half into the center of each cookie and bake for 10 to 12 minutes.

ESTIMATED PREPARATION TIME: 10 minutes.

ESTIMATED COOKING TIME: 20 to 40 minutes.

HIGH ALTITUDE NOTE: Increase oven temperature to 400 degrees.

69 Calories
0.7 g Protein
9.6 g Carbohydrates
3.3 g Fat
0.4 g Fiber
34 mg Sodium
2 mg Cholesterol

Busy Mom's Lowfat Cookbook

Quick Mincemeat Turnovers

Yield: 8 servings

Preheat oven to 425 degrees. Lightly coat a nonstick cookie sheet with cooking oil spray. Unroll crescent roll dough and separate triangles. Lightly brush one side of 8 triangles with skim milk and place on cookie sheet, milk side up. Place a heaping tablespoon of mincemeat in the center of each of the 8 prepared triangles. Carefully align the remaining triangles, placing one on the top of each of the filled triangles. Using the tines of a fork, press triangle edges together to seal. Brush lightly with remaining milk and bake for 8 to 10 minutes.

2 cans (7½ ounces each) crescent roll dough
¼ cup skim milk
1½ cups prepared mincemeat

ESTIMATED PREPARATION TIME: 15 minutes.

ESTIMATED COOKING TIME: 8 minutes.

269 Calories
3.9 g Protein
40.0 g Carbohydrates
12.4 g Fat
2.6 g Fiber
506 mg Sodium
0 mg Cholesterol

Hamantaschen

Yield: about 4 dozen cookies

½ cup sugar
¼ cup canola oil
2 tablespoons margarine, softened
1 egg
1 teaspoon pure vanilla
2 cups flour
1 teaspoon baking powder
pinch of salt
½ cup apricot preserves
½ cup prune preserves

Place sugar, oil, and margarine in a large mixing bowl. Using an electric mixer on medium speed, beat until smooth. Add egg and continue mixing until smooth. Blend in vanilla. In a separate bowl, mix flour, baking powder, and salt until well combined. Stir the flour mixture into the sugar mixture until just blended. Gather the dough into a ball, wrap with plastic wrap, flatten slightly, and refrigerate for 2 to 3 hours.

Preheat oven to 350 degrees. Divide dough in half, returning one half to refrigerator. On a lightly floured work surface, roll dough to a thickness of ⅛ inch. Using a drinking glass, cut circles out of dough. Place ½ teaspoon of preserves in the center of each dough circle. Turn edges of each circle up to partially cover filling, forming a 3-cornered cookie, and pinch the corners to hold shape. Place cookies about 1½ inches apart on a nonstick cookie sheet and bake for 10 to 15 minutes, or until golden brown. Cool on racks. Repeat with remaining dough.

77 Calories
0.7 g Protein
15.1 g Carbohydrates
1.7 g Fat
0.2 g Fiber
17 mg Sodium
4 mg Cholesterol

ESTIMATED PREPARATION TIME: 20 to 30 minutes plus refrigeration time.

ESTIMATED COOKING TIME: 20 to 30 minutes.

Busy Mom's Lowfat Cookbook

Passover Matzo Layer Cake

Yield: 10 servings

Place sugar and chocolate in a medium nonstick pot. Add 1 cup water. Bring to boil over low heat, stirring constantly. Add the canola oil and halvah, and continue stirring until the liquid begins to bubble. Briefly remove from burner.

Dissolve cornstarch in remaining 2 tablespoons of water, and add to chocolate mixture. Return pot to burner and stir until mixture thickens. Remove from heat. Stir in Kosher red wine.

Place a matzo on a large serving platter. Spread a thin layer of chocolate on the top. Place another matzo over that one, and continue to layer, finishing with a chocolate layer. Chill for at least one hour.

¼ cup sugar
4 ounces unsweetened chocolate
1 cup plus 2 tablespoons water
¼ cup canola oil
6 ounces halvah, diced
2 tablespoons cornstarch
½ cup Kosher red wine
6 large matzos

ESTIMATED PREPARATION TIME: 20 minutes (plus 1 hour to chill).

ESTIMATED COOKING TIME: 15 minutes.

298 Calories
6.2 g Protein
31.5 g Carbohydrates
15.8 g Fat
1.1 g Fiber
2 mg Sodium
0 mg Cholesterol

Orange Chicken (Kosher)

Yield: 6 servings

3 pounds boneless,
   skinless chicken
   breasts
1 tablespoon canola oil
1 lemon
2 oranges
½ teaspoon salt
1 teaspoon minced garlic
1 teaspoon chili powder
2 teaspoons paprika
1 teaspoon coriander

Preheat oven to 375 degrees. Brown the chicken breasts in the canola oil in a large nonstick skillet. Remove and place in a 13- × 9-inch baking dish.

Slice lemon in half and juice one half, reserving juice in a small bowl. Slice the other half into rounds. Juice one of the oranges, reserving juice with the lemon juice. Slice the other orange into rounds. Add the seasonings to the citrus juices and stir. Pour over chicken. Arrange lemon and orange slices on top and bake for 20 minutes.

ESTIMATED PREPARATION TIME: 15 minutes.

ESTIMATED COOKING TIME: 25 minutes.

329 Calories
54.0 g Protein
5.9 g Carbohydrates
8.8 g Fat
0.9 g Fiber
308 mg Sodium
146 mg Cholesterol

Busy Mom's Lowfat Cookbook

Sugar-and-Cinnamon Passover Cookies (Kosher)

Yield: about 3 dozen cookies

Preheat oven to 350 degrees. In a medium mixing bowl, combine almonds, cinnamon, and sugar. In a separate bowl, using an electric mixer, beat egg whites until stiff. Gently fold beaten egg whites into sugar mixture. Lightly coat a nonstick cookie sheet with cooking oil spray. Take teaspoonfuls of dough, gently form into balls, and place on cookie sheet about 1½ inches apart. Bake for 25 minutes. Place powdered sugar in a small bowl, and roll warm cookies in sugar, coating evenly. Place cookies on a rack to cool.

Note: These cookies are very sweet, and should be eaten in moderation.

1 cup ground almonds
1½ tablespoons cinnamon
1 cup sugar
2 egg whites
1 cup powdered sugar

ESTIMATED PREPARATION TIME: 25 minutes.

ESTIMATED COOKING TIME: 25 minutes.

150 Calories
5.0 g Protein
7.7 g Carbohydrates
12.2 g Fat
2.6 g Fiber
6 mg Sodium
0 mg Cholesterol

Sunny Orange Rolls

Yield: 10 to 12

2 cups flour (or 1 cup white flour plus 1 cup whole wheat flour)
¼ cup sugar
1 tablespoon baking powder
¼ teaspoon salt
1 tablespoon canola oil
½ cup skim milk
½ cup "lite" orange marmalade
½ cup powdered sugar
1 tablespoon orange juice

Preheat oven to 400 degrees. In a medium bowl, combine the first 4 ingredients and stir with a fork. Add the oil and stir vigorously until the mixture resembles bread crumbs. Add milk and mix well. The dough should be easy to handle. If not, add flour one teaspoon at a time until you can form a ball with it.

Place dough between 2 sheets of waxed paper, and pat or roll out to approximately ½ inch thick. Spread marmalade on the dough, and roll the dough tightly to form a tube. Cut roll into 1-inch round slices with a sharp knife, and place in a 13- × 9-inch baking dish that has been lightly coated with cooking oil spray.

Bake for 15 minutes. Remove from oven and cool slightly.

In a small bowl, combine powdered sugar and orange juice, stirring vigorously until smooth and creamy. Drizzle over rolls.

157 Calories
2.5 g Protein
33.2 g Carbohydrates
1.5 g Fat
0.6 g Fiber
76 mg Sodium
0 mg Cholesterol

ESTIMATED PREPARATION TIME: 15 minutes.

ESTIMATED COOKING TIME: 15 minutes.

HIGH ALTITUDE NOTE: Increase oven temperature to 425 degrees.

Busy Mom's Lowfat Cookbook

Easter Raspberry Cheesecake

Yield: 6 to 8 servings

Preheat oven to 350 degrees. Place cream cheese, sugar, egg substitute, sour cream, and almond extract in a large mixing bowl and beat until smooth. Add flour and beat until blended. Fold in 1 cup of the berries. Pour into pie shell and bake for 35 minutes. Allow to cool, then chill for at least 1 hour. Garnish with remaining berries.

ESTIMATED PREPARATION TIME: 10 minutes (plus 1 hour to chill).

ESTIMATED COOKING TIME: 35 minutes.

1 brick (12 ounces) nonfat cream cheese, softened
1 cup sugar
½ cup egg substitute
½ cup fat-free sour cream
¼ teaspoon almond extract
¼ cup flour
2 cups raspberries (fresh or frozen)
1 prepared chocolate cookie pie crust

317 Calories
10.4 g Protein
48.8 g Carbohydrates
9.2 g Fat
1.0 g Fiber
480 mg Sodium
8 mg Cholesterol

Easy Rack-of-Lamb Dinner

Yield: 8 servings

3-pound lamb crown
    roast, prepared by
    butcher into rack
8 small new potatoes
1 package (16 ounces)
    frozen baby carrots
1 cup water
2 teaspoons dried crushed
    mint leaves
    salt and pepper
1 package (10 ounces)
    frozen peas and pearl
    onions, thawed

Preheat oven to 325 degrees. Place rack of lamb in center of a shallow roasting pan. Place potatoes in the center of the rack of lamb. Arrange carrots around the sides of the rack of lamb and pour water over vegetables. Sprinkle meat with crushed mint leaves, salt, and pepper. Bake for 30 minutes, then add peas and onions. Bake for an additional 15 minutes. Remove from oven and place rack of lamb on a large serving platter. Garnish with cooked vegetables and serve.

ESTIMATED PREPARATION TIME: 10 minutes.

ESTIMATED COOKING TIME: 45 minutes.

410 Calories
37.7 g Protein
39.9 g Carbohydrates
10.7 g Fat
3.3 g Fiber
175 mg Sodium
103 mg Cholesterol

Easy Hot Cross Buns

Yield: 12 rolls

Prepare roll dough according to package directions, adding raisins and nutmeg to dough. Pull dough into 12 equal pieces and shape each into a ball. Place about 2 inches apart on a nonstick cookie sheet. Snip a cross on the top of each ball with kitchen scissors, cover, and let rise about 1 hour.

Preheat oven to 375 degrees. Brush tops of buns with egg white and bake for 20 minutes. Allow to cool. In a small bowl, mix powdered sugar, water, and vanilla, then brush mixture over buns.

1 package (14½ ounce tube) roll mix
¾ cup raisins
¼ teaspoon nutmeg
1 egg white, slightly beaten
¾ cup powdered sugar
2 teaspoons water
¼ teaspoon vanilla

ESTIMATED PREPARATION TIME: 15 minutes plus 1 hour rising time.

ESTIMATED COOKING TIME: 20 minutes.

177 Calories
4.0 g Protein
37.1 g Carbohydrates
1.2 g Fat
1.6 g Fiber
234 mg Sodium
0 mg Cholesterol

Independence Cake

Yield: 16 servings

1 purchased pound cake, cut in thirds horizontally
4 cups raspberries
1⅓ cups blueberries
1 tub (12 ounces) reduced-fat nondairy whipped topping, thawed

Line bottom of 13- × 9-inch baking pan with pound cake slices. Top with 1½ cups of the raspberries, 1 cup of the blueberries and the entire contents of the tub of whipped topping.

Place remaining raspberries and blueberries on the whipped topping in a flag design. Refrigerate until ready to serve.

ESTIMATED PREPARATION TIME: 15 minutes.

149 Calories
1.4 g Protein
19.9 g Carbohydrates
9.5 g Fat
1.2 g Fiber
81 mg Sodium
21 mg Cholesterol

Grilled Buffalo Burgers

Yield: 5 servings

Light charcoal in a grill. In a medium bowl, combine buffalo meat, onion, chili powder, and pepper. Mix thoroughly. Divide into 5 equal portions and form patties.

Place on grill over hot coals and brush with Worcestershire sauce. Grill for 5 to 10 minutes, occasionally brushing with sauce. Turn burgers once and grill for 2 to 3 minutes, or until buffalo is medium-well-done, occasionally brushing with sauce. Serve on rolls with condiments of your choice.

1¼ pounds ground buffalo
¼ cup finely chopped onion
½ teaspoon chili powder
⅛ teaspoon pepper
¼ cup Worcestershire sauce
5 split whole wheat Kaiser rolls

ESTIMATED PREPARATION TIME: 5 minutes.

ESTIMATED COOKING TIME: 12 minutes.

268 Calories
37.5 g Protein
19.8 g Carbohydrates
4.3 g Fat
3.2 g Fiber
358 mg Sodium
36 mg Cholesterol

Summer Pasta Salad

Yield: 6 servings

3 cups cooked spiral
  pasta twirls
¾ cup chopped fresh
  tomato
⅔ cup chopped cucumber
½ cup chopped yellow bell
  pepper
⅓ cup chopped green
  onions
⅓ cup chopped ripe olives
¼ cup light vinaigrette
  dressing

Place all ingredients in a large bowl. Toss until well combined, cover, and chill.

ESTIMATED PREPARATION TIME: 20 minutes.

126 Calories
3.9 g Protein
23.9 g Carbohydrates
1.7 g Fat
2.2 g Fiber
238 mg Sodium
0 mg Cholesterol

Busy Mom's Lowfat Cookbook

Index